PRAISE FOR

America Calling

"Anyone who has wondered about the modern immigrant experience and perceptions of coming to this nation to fulfill dreams will find *America Calling* a lesson in adaptation, advantage, and revised futures."

—*Midwest Book Review*

"*America Calling* is a timely and unique addition to immigrant literature. Bhandari weaves an evocative and compelling narrative of the power of education to connect and transform—an experience that resonates deeply with me as a first-generation immigrant and college student."

—**Reyna Grande**, award-winning author of *A Dream Called Home* and *The Distance Between Us*

"Rajika Bhandari is a voice that urges us with moral clarity and rigorous intelligence . . . this is a clarion call for the nation's policymakers and educators to welcome all curious minds."

—**Maeve Higgins**, *New York Times* columnist, award-winning author of *Maeve in America: Essays by a Girl from Somewhere*

"Through this intimate account of her own journey, Rajika Bhandari tells the story of the millions of young people who pursue the dream of an American education . . . and the often misunderstood, underappreciated yet immense value they bring about. While she grew up in Delhi and I in Madrid, her story is, in many ways, mine too."

—**Angel Cabrera**, president, Georgia Institute of Technology (Georgia Tech) and a Carnegie Corporation "Great Immigrant"

"By turns analytical and heartfelt, *America Calling* is an engaging and timely read that will resonate strongly amongst the global academic community. . . . As an immigrant with an educational background that spans two continents myself, I see an element of universality in Bhandari's narrative that transcends culture and national origin."

—**Andrew Hamilton**, president of New York University and former vice-chancellor, University of Oxford

"Dr. Rajika Bhandari starts with her personal journey and broadens out to support a universal truth: The US is better off with the rich diversity and expertise brought by international students to American campuses and society. A touching and insightful must-read."
—**Lenora Chu,** Chinese education expert and award-winning author of *Little Soldiers: An American Boy, a Chinese School and the Global Race to Achieve*

"Rajika explains why the world's brightest flock to American shores and boost its competitiveness—and why they are now returning home. She is right that if America doesn't correct the exodus, it will be the greater loser."
—**Vivek Wadhwa,** distinguished fellow, Harvard Law School, Labor and Worklife Program, best-selling author of *The Immigrant Exodus*

"Rajika Bhandari offers a roadmap to the many who have come, and the many who will be drawn to America. It is deeply personal and yet illustrative of the many shared experiences of generations that continue to enrich a nation built by and for immigrants."
—**Raju Narisetti,** founder of *Mint* newspaper, and former managing editor at *The Washington Post* and *The Wall Street Journal*

"A rich testament to the importance of international students, *America Calling* is also an important addition to the story of the Indian diaspora in the US."
—**Devesh Kapur,** Starr Foundation professor of South Asian Studies, Johns Hopkins School of Advanced International Studies and award-winning co-author of *The Other One Percent: Indians in America*

"*America Calling* is a one-of-a-kind book, relevant to both students and educators all over the world. The US remains one of the most sought-after destinations for tertiary education, and Rajika's book is a tremendous contribution to the literature on this global trend."
—**Pramath Raj Sinha,** founding dean of Indian School of Business and co-founder of Ashoka University

"Seeking an international education takes courage, as Cervantes reminds us. But it's not a quixotic venture. As Dr Bhandari 's story illustrates, the windmills of the mind can be overcome, and the arc of educational exchange bends toward open doors and open minds."
—**Allan E. Goodman,** President and CEO, Institute of International Education (IIE)

AMERICA CALLING

A Foreign Student in a
Country of Possibility

Rajika Bhandari

SHE WRITES PRESS

Published 2021
Printed in the United States of America
Print ISBN: 978-1-64742-183-0
E-ISBN: 978-1-64742-184-7
Library of Congress Control Number: 2021905883

For information, address:
She Writes Press
1569 Solano Ave #546
Berkeley, CA 94707

She Writes Press is a division of SparkPoint Studio, LLC.

Book design by Stacey Aaronson

All company and/or product names may be trade names, logos, trademarks, and/or registered trademarks and are the property of their respective owners.

Names and identifying characteristics have been changed to protect the privacy of certain individuals.

For my mother who gave me the wings to fly
and my daughter who inspires me to keep moving
forward, and for the millions of students around the
world who venture abroad, dreaming and taking risks

Contents

Author's Note

To write this book, I relied on my memory and interpretation of events, on my professional knowledge and scholarship about international students, and on relevant data and research. Certain events are omitted to preserve narrative flow. The names of most individuals and other identifying information have been changed to protect privacy. The resemblance of these altered names to individuals—living or dead—is purely coincidental. There are no composite characters in the book.

Prologue

They arrive in the US each August, thousands of them with dreams in their eyes and nervousness in their hearts, their belongings usually contained in just two suitcases. They come from over two hundred countries, large metropolises, and small towns—from China to Saudi Arabia, from Taipei to Timbuktu— heading to college campuses all over America, big Ivy Leagues and small community colleges, in New York City, Mobile, Alabama, and points in between. You can spot them easily at any of America's major airports, as they emerge from the belly of the airplane in twos or threes; perhaps their parents knew each other and made sure they had company on their travels over to a foreign land. Or perhaps they befriended each other somewhere along the way, embarking on a shared journey to a country that was strange yet familiar thanks to television and the internet.

Their luggage contains all their belongings, which will have to suffice until they can make enough money to buy clothes in America. That could take a while. The suitcases are bulging with clothes, books, homemade snacks in carefully sealed packets, and perhaps even a pressure cooker for the ambitious cook. Big white labels pasted on to the suitcases proclaim the travelers' long and strange names and their US destinations. For now, these are the maps of their lives: where they have come from and where they are going. But even on that first journey, their identity begins to get truncated as the address labels get ripped apart in hold of the airplane. So Deepesh is now just Deep and _____ becomes Ash, convenient nicknames that their American friends will use anyway as their real ones are simply too much of a mouthful.

These travelers are foreign or international students who seek an American university degree, the Made-in-America brand prized by students all over the world. Their burdens are not light. They carry with them not only their two suitcases, but also their personal and professional aspirations, and the hopes and dreams of generations.

My journey as an international student began in 1992, just like that of the thousands of students who arrive at the doorstep of America each fall. I arrived from India, one of 439,000 international students in America that year. Back then, as a newly arrived doctoral student in psychology, I could never have imagined that many years later I would study with the objectivity of a detached researcher the very migration that I had been a part of. That I would one day be immersed in the current debates that surround foreign students and the value of immigrants, the value of learning from outsiders—arguments and issues that are at once personal, for I have lived through many of them, yet are political, with implications for our nation and the world.

Speaking to students, teachers, and administrators at many of the American campuses that host international students as well as to everyday Americans from North Carolina to California to New York and everywhere in between, I've realized that Americans do not truly understand the experiences of international students in the US; their value to the US; or the nexus between education, global talent, and immigration on which the future of America hinges. For the average American, there is simply no understanding of the central role that international students—especially those who become immigrants—play in the arc of American prosperity and success.

To most, an international student is just the college classmate with an accent whom your son or daughter brings home for Thanksgiving or is the Chinese kid who might be taking away a college seat from a deserving American student. But beyond these stereotypes, international students remain a mysterious and foreign group. Yet they are everywhere—1.1 million of them spread across almost four thousand campuses, living in small college towns in middle America and in large cities on the two coasts. They are the invisible and unacknowledged drivers of the massive engine of American higher education that depends on them, bringing in $45 billion to the US economy each year and helping to create four hundred thousand jobs.

When I began to write this book, I was afraid that my experiences would be dated. My own experience as an international student in the US had begun almost a quarter century ago. So much had changed since then: the Twin Towers had fallen and stock markets had ebbed and flowed; hulking computers had been replaced with handheld gizmos; digital notebooks had replaced actual ones; students were now customers being wooed by different countries as opposed to grateful recipients of the largesse of rich countries; national boundaries had been drawn and redrawn; and everything about the landscape of higher education itself had changed.

Yet, as I spoke to student after student while researching this book, I was struck by how much has remained the same, especially a student and family's aspiration for a better education as the ticket to a successful future and the learning and growth that come from expanding one's geographic and mental boundaries. But the struggles have also remained the same: the academic, social, and cultural challenges on campus and beyond; the struggle to survive financially; the feeling of not being able to breathe, of suffocation and fear when navigating a maze of immigration policies as a "nonresident alien"; of purportedly being among America's best and brightest, yet having one's existence and presence questioned every step of the way.

But what had also endured over time was the appeal of America. Being able to study in America represents not just a world-class education, but also freedom of thought, the ability to pursue one's own unique version of the American dream in a land of milk and honey. As one Chinese female student told me: "Coming to America for me was not just about studying and accumulating wealth. It made me audacious . . . I felt I could do the impossible. Only in America is this possible."

I heard this idea repeated often, by students, by Silicon Valley entrepreneurs, by university founders in India whose experiences in the US helped shape their future vision, by ambassadors who recognized the role that education plays in building relationships with other countries when all other policy levers fail, and by brilliant young scientists and trailblazers who still believe in America but were forced to leave because the country's immigration system shut the door on them.

One thing is clear: the idea of an American education is powerful, etched in the psychology of developing countries like India where it is often assumed that West is the best, where the notion of Western superiority—be it in embracing canned food and milk powder, Western medical practices or systems of education—is deeply ingrained in the postcolonial Indian consciousness. Where

Indians like my grandfather once aspired to an Oxbridge education, students of my generation turned to America. But what did
not change was that we all continued to look westwards. Today,
too, eighty-five years after my grandfather set sail from India to
study in England, over three hundred thousand Indian students
travel to the West for an education, with most of them heading to
the US.

I also learned how education is deeply connected to immigration, to the very definition of success in America. My experience and that of the million students who come to the US has
also been the pathway for much of America's global talent,
whether it was Nobel Prize laureates or doctors working in a
rural part of the country, or Kamala Harris's parents who arrived
in the US as international students—her mother from India and
her father from Jamaica. The relationship between the US and
the world depends on this flow of education and knowledge, a
delicate dance in which other countries sometimes give more
and the US leads and other times when other countries gain
more and the US cedes, but in which each needs the other.

America's gain from the journey from education to immigration—the recipe for the country's prosperity and competitiveness—has existed for the past two hundred years, yet the
pathway between the two has become increasingly broken, especially during the Trump administration, which dealt blow after
blow to international students. Students around the world—
America's future talent and its best global ambassadors—are
now asking: Do we even want to study in America?

International students vote with their feet. Armed with information from the internet and wooed by recruiters around the
world, they are savvy consumers with a focus on the return on

investment of a foreign degree. They assess their options carefully, comparing destination countries as vastly different as the US and China. In short, students have more choices than ever before. America's recent losses in attracting global talent have been a gain for other competing countries, like Canada whose loosening of immigration restrictions coincided fortuitously with Trump's election in November 2016.

It is exactly times like these, when there has been growing nationalism and xenophobia and a contentious debate about who should stay and who should leave, that underscore why America needs to keep its minds and doors open, where American students also benefit from studying alongside students from Syria or Nigeria. Only one out of ten American undergraduates will study abroad, but the presence of an international student in American classrooms provides some global exposure for the remaining 90 percent of American students who do not have the opportunity to venture outside their country or even their cities.

When I came to America, the long and complex history of race relations in the US was a revelation to me, as was the extent of the Holocaust, which had received just a passing reference in my history textbooks in India. On the other hand, my American friends learned for the first time about the tragic partition of India and Pakistan and that it caused what is arguably the largest human exodus in modern history. America's famed and sought-after Ivy Leagues—each of which hosts several thousand international students—retain their appeal and their global rankings in large part because of the international learning environment they are able to offer American students and others from all over the world.

⌒⌒

INTERNATIONAL STUDENTS leave their homes to travel long distances for many reasons. Most, especially Asians, look westwards to attain the ideal of a foreign degree; many others, such as European students, are less clear-eyed about a return on investment on their education and are motivated instead by the cultural goals of exchange and immersion. Still others want to come but are deterred by the growing gun violence in the US and the fear of visa denials or, worse yet, are stopped at the border even with a valid visa in hand.

But there is one overwhelming reason that students move to another country, yet it is one that is never documented or discussed seriously lest it appear too frivolous when measured against grander aspirations. No survey of the motivations of international students has ever asked them whether they moved because they were following the arc of their romantic relationship. And those who leave and follow for this reason are usually young women, who almost universally are socialized to be the followers rather than the leaders when it comes to the trajectory of their relationships, allowing the pursuit of romance to shape their personal and professional dreams. This common cultural pattern was part of my own story as well.

In many ways, I was an accidental international student and an accidental immigrant; I never deliberately planned to become either. Like countless others before me, I came to the US following a relationship that formed the foundation of my early years in the US as an international student. But while I might have come to America as a naive twenty-one-year-old woman following in the footsteps of a man, I soon forged my own path that was ultimately shaped by America. As is true for students and all young people all over the world, an educational journey is not just about academic learning but also about finding one's place in the world of where one eventually belongs. For me, this place —this new home—eventually came to be America.

Emigrating from one's homeland is never an easy decision or one made casually. While for me it meant embracing all the opportunities in America, a country of possibility, it also meant erasing in a fundamental way the contours of my life's existence and a reality that defines each of us—my citizenship. But in every choice made in life, there is something lost and something gained. I lost the ability to vote in India, but I gained the right to vote for America's first Black president and its first Indian American woman vice president, whose legacy is itself a testament to what international students and immigrants bring to America. For other international students, the choice has been a return to their original home country, or even a third country. These migrants with mortarboards seek and pursue opportunities where they exist, but also give back to that land they journey to, however fleeting the time spent there.

Even though international students are part of the fabric of American higher education and the history of immigrant America, their stories are rarely told. Why do they need America, and why does America need them? This is a book about one such story—my story and my personal journey as an international student, as a woman, and as an immigrant. It was a journey through which I learned to walk straighter, to speak louder, and to think for myself.

PART I

You get a strange feeling when you're about to leave a place . . . like you'll not only miss the people you love but you'll miss the person you are now at this time and this place, because you'll never be this way ever again.

—AZAR NAFISI,
Reading Lolita in Tehran: A Memoir in Books

1

Two Suitcases

I felt tiny on the stage of the large auditorium as I looked up at the two hundred young freshmen who stared back at me. The glare of the lights hurt my eyes, but I could discern row after row of mostly white faces as they looked at me expectantly. Some sat slouched in their seats, their baseball hats cocked to the side, while others leaned forward, tapping their pencils impatiently on their notepads. It was 1:00 p.m. on a Tuesday, eastern standard time. I had arrived in Raleigh, North Carolina, from India less than forty-eight hours ago, traveling across two oceans and 8,500 miles. I had yet to find a place to live. But here I stood, before these American students, as they and I sized each other up.

My heartbeat pounded in my ears, my mouth was dry, and I felt a telltale flush rising from my neck to my face. They were waiting, as was the professor in the wings of the auditorium. I forced a smile, took a deep breath, and pulled back my shoulders. I positioned myself behind the mike at the podium.

"Good morning. Welcome to Introduction to Psychology 101. Dr. Broussard is your professor, but I'm your teaching assistant, Rajika Bhandari." Perhaps it was my imagination, but I detected a collective eye roll: *Great, we're stuck with a TA with an accent.*

I pushed on.

"I'll play a brief recording for you. Based on what you hear, please write down three things you associate with the voice." Professor Broussard liked to start the semester in a dramatic and unexpected way and had chosen to begin his first class with a small experiment in social psychology that revealed how we often form judgments about people based on their voices and accents. It had fallen to me to introduce the students to the class. I turned away from the mike, went into the wings, and pressed "play" on the audio-visual console. The tape began to run, and the professor's stentorian voice boomed through the auditorium's speakers. I watched the students listening carefully to the disembodied voice, trying to fit an image to the words. And I couldn't help but wonder what first impressions the students had formed of me. I wondered how I appeared to them in my carefully selected outfit of purple culottes, a printed cotton top, and my green suede flats, a young and foreign woman just a few years older than most of them.

FORTY-EIGHT HOURS AGO, Vikram and I had left Delhi on an American Airlines flight that departed at 2:00 a.m. from Indira Gandhi International Airport. On the drive to the airport in my aunt's white Maruti Omni van, I clutched my mother's hand and counted the highway signs as they brought me closer and closer to the terminal. The only other vehicles on the road were the lumbering trucks traveling inter-state and people like us, headed to the airport to put themselves or their loved ones on a plane that would transport them thousands of miles away.

The van pulled up outside the departure terminal. Only passengers were allowed inside for security reasons. But Vikram's family was connected in ways that mattered in Delhi, and his parents had managed to arrange special permits for themselves and my mother to enter the airport building. Vikram and his parents met us near the Air India counter where we were to check in. I pressed my mother's hand, though I don't know what I was reassuring her about. My mother was used to these sorts of moments, alone in her times of joy and sadness. I had seen my father the day before, dutifully visiting him before my departure for America. He made a half-hearted overture to come to the airport, but I insisted that he not put himself through the trouble.

The only other people at the terminal were the female janitors in their khaki *salwar* suit uniforms, mopping the airport floor, and the passengers waiting with their families, the tears in their eyes now replaced with the emotional and physical exhaustion of staying up all night. The sterile, white glow of the fluorescent tube lights didn't help. At that unearthly hour there was no daylight to make everything seem just a little bit less sad, less final.

For the journey I dressed in what I imagined a smart, westward-bound student might wear—faded jeans and a red shirt with a scarf—and I carried a tote bag with a blue paisley print. My two large suitcases, the maximum allowed by the airline, were now checked in. My mother and I had bought them just some weeks ago from the Kings Store in Bhopal. "Madam, first-class," the owner had said, giving us a thumbs-up sign, assuring us that the suitcases would stand up to the rigor of a transcontinental flight. We had spent the past month carefully amassing the things I might need in America that could be contained in just two pieces of luggage. There were the clothes that I thought would suit a young, Indian graduate student in the US: jeans, tops, cotton skirts, and dresses bought from Janpath—the market where Delhi's fashion-conscious college students flocked to buy samples of western clothes rejected by designer labels. Then there was the tailoring of the Indian clothes for which I had first bought matching fabric from the bazaar and then spent many patient mornings with our tailor, Hamid, to whom we still gave our business despite his age, his unsteady hands, and his failing eyesight. For special occasions, my mother carefully selected five silk saris with their matching blouses and petticoats. And then there was Parachute coconut hair oil, packets of henna for my hair, Shahnaz Hussain's herbal beauty products, dried fruits and nuts, and spices. We bought and packed enough to last me a year, which is when I planned to be back.

All the packing and planning had led up to the night before, which I spent clinging to my mother like a baby, inhaling her unique scent tinged with the Pond's sandalwood talcum powder she had used for years. But now with our bags checked and boarding passes issued, it was time for our final goodbyes. Vikram touched his parents' feet to seek their blessings; I hugged my mother tightly. By the time I left India that night, my mother and I were used to our frequent partings—I had spent a large part of my twenty-one years away from home in boarding schools that offered a better-quality education and then at a top university in the large metropolis of Delhi.

Yet going away to America was different. For the first time, we would be separated by almost ten thousand miles and different time zones, a chasm that we promised to bridge through phone calls and letters. I had often waved goodbye to my mother, my face and raised hand framed in the rectangular and grimy windows of trains and buses, but this time it was at the final immigration barrier in the airport.

I turned back for a last glimpse of her anxious face, not knowing when I might see her again, knowing only that the next time I spoke to her she would be a disembodied voice at the end of a telephone line half a world away. She would be here—in India—and I would be there—in America—and there was very little in between that could change that indelible truth.

UP UNTIL THE AGE of eighteen, I had no desire to leave India to study in the US. My father had tried his best to get me to consider it, my resistance matched in equal measure by his insistence. On a hot summer morning in 1990 in Bombay, when I was visiting my father during my summer break, he decided to take matters into his own hands and to find out more about sending me to America to study. I accompanied him reluctantly as we started out from his flat in the Church Gate area of the city and wended our way through the early morning rush hour crowd. Hundreds of people poured out of the main entrance of the Church Gate station, like worker ants on a mission. I stuck close to my father as we zigzagged from one intersection to the next, making our way to the United States Educational Foundation of India (now known as the United States India Educational Foundation), or the Fulbright Commission. There, we sat under the rotations of a slow ceiling fan, flipping through page after page of US university brochures and directories, each one proclaiming itself as the "best" for this and the "top" for that. My father jotted down some information, purchased international aerogrammes, and pain-stakingly wrote to a whole bunch of universities that he thought might be willing to admit me. I don't recall the details of what he said in those letters, or who exactly he sent them to. What I do know is that he spent a lot on the postage and that I had no interest in any of it.

I was afraid that if I left to go study in America, I would be faced with a difficult choice after finishing my studies: remain in the US and join the ranks of Indian immigrants there, or return home to India. I had often heard that being a foreigner in the US was like being a fly trapped in honey. America tempted and en-snared you, and yet when you wanted to leave, you discovered you couldn't. In India everything seemed preordained: you went to school, you studied hard, got a good percentage in your twelfth grade exit exams, and then tried to get into a good col-lege. One didn't question this sequence, ever. This is what the generation before me had done and this is what was expected of me. I was not used to having choices and, from what I had heard, America represented too much choice and too many decisions. Even when it came to selecting a college or university in the US, there were over four thousand to choose from. To go or not to go? To stay or not to stay? Best not to go, I concluded.

And yet, just two years later, here I was, plotting and plan-ning my move to America. If my earlier reluctance to go to America was based on emotion and fear, the decision to come to America was also one based on emotion, but a different one. When the heart got involved, the decision to leave India and follow Vikram and the destiny of my relationship (which seemed westward-bound) suddenly came easily to me.

Vikram and I first met when we were in different high schools —he in twelfth grade and I in tenth grade. My boarding school was up in the hills, and his school was in Delhi. I met him at a picnic where I tagged along with my aunt who was his history teacher, and whom I was visiting during my winter vacations. Vikram charmed me with his guitar and his soulful voice as we all gathered around him under a tree, singing along to favorites by John Denver and Peter, Paul and Mary. I was smitten, but there was not much I could do. Apart from the geographic distance, there was also the inconvenient fact that he had a girlfriend then.

We soon lost touch and would reconnect many years later when, through common friends, he managed to trace me. We quickly fell in love, a meant-to-be romance that had awaited its turn for three years. In the fashion of many other whirlwind relationships, we were soon engaged. Our aspirations were one, or rather his aspirations became mine. And his dream, like that of many other young Indians, was to come to America to study computer science.

Vikram left for the US in 1991, heading to North Carolina State University, and the plan was that I was to join him the following year. I waited eagerly for Vikram's letters from North Carolina which arrived every few days, the long sheets of yellow, lined paper neatly folded and stuffed into crisp white envelopes with stamps bearing the American flag. I imagined Vikram sitting alone at the desk in his bedroom as I read the letters in which he guided me through the process of where to apply, where to get more information, what to say in my essays. Clear-eyed and determined, I quickly immersed myself in the vocabulary of America-bound students—the Graduate Record Examination (GRE), the Test of English as a Foreign Language (TOEFL), the personal essay, and the F-1 student visa—all of which I had eschewed just two years ago despite my father's best attempts.

I struggled most with the personal essay. I had written essays many things before, summarizing information into compelling arguments, but had never been taught how to write an essay about myself, let alone one where I had to convince someone ten thousand miles away that I deserved admission to their university. The notion of writing about myself, my motivations and my plans, was alien to me. I had never particularly questioned why I was studying psychology and had drifted into it like many of my classmates. It had boiled down to a process of elimination rather than being a carefully calibrated decision.

In high school I had always been artistic and a strong writer, editor of my school magazine. My English teacher, Dr. Dhillon, was convinced that I would go on to become a writer or a journalist, following in the footsteps of my father. But the pragmatist in me triumphed. I had observed firsthand through my father the peripatetic reality of a journalistic life and had determined early on that it wasn't for me. I turned my back on artistic or writing endeavors as neither seemed to promise a stable livelihood. On the other hand, there was English literature, which I loved, but which my mother—herself a professor of English—dissuaded me from as the only viable career option was teaching, which in India seemed to be the last resort of many rather than the first choice of a select few.

So, with all these options eliminated, what did that leave me with? Most respectable girls those days would go into the humanities or the social sciences, and so I opted for psychology, a solid and safe bet that promised some job prospects. But this didn't seem like a compelling enough argument to make in a personal essay. I instead wrote an essay about lofty goals that looked good on paper, but which I felt nervous I wouldn't be able to live up to.

Then there were the GRE and the TOEFL. I prepared well for both, soaking up the thick books and practice tests that Vikram had sent me from the US. I was nervous about the GRE. My math had never been good, and the Advanced GRE assumed that I had studied psychology for four years. But my undergraduate degree had taken only three years, like most Indian degrees since they were modeled on the British system. I played catch-up with the GRE material, teaching myself child psychology from textbooks. Many questions on the GRE general test stumped me. I didn't know that a baseball field was called a diamond; I knew nothing about baseball. I would learn only later about the well-known cultural bias of the GRE, leading international students to often score higher on the quantitative portion of the GRE as compared with American students, and slightly lower on the verbal and analytical portions.

The toughness of the GRE was made up for by the pointlessness of the TOEFL, where I sat for an hour with headphones as a man's voice with an American accent intoned sentence after sentence in a soporific voice. The grammatical errors to be identified in the test were obvious. I had been speaking English since I was a child and, in many ways, it was my first language. Of course, I would be able to tell the difference between when to use "they" and when to use "them."

I applied to five universities, all in North Carolina so that I could be close to Vikram. I worried about whether I would receive financial help in the form of a teaching assistantship, without which I could not have come to the US—it was simply too expensive. In 1991, the year before I had applied to study in the US, several girls in my hostel in Delhi had received offers of admission from top universities like Harvard and Yale but eventually were unable to go because of a recession that had forced US institutions to cut scholarships for international students.

North Carolina State University—my top pick—first offered me admission but without aid and I was added to a wait list for an assistantship. I felt deflated and weary, and uncertain of my future. But then a month later I received a letter from the university that informed me that one of the students admitted with aid dropped out and a spot had opened for me. It felt like sheer luck.

Now, armed with all the necessary paperwork from my future university, it was time to apply for my F-1 visa at the US Embassy in Delhi. Situated within the diplomatic enclave of Chanakyapuri, a part of Delhi named after the ancient thinker and diplomat, Chanakya, the US Embassy was the most protected building in the city, a sprawling modern 1950s-era building surrounded by barricades and security men. To know the appeal of America, the land of the free and home of the brave, one had only to look at the crowds that gathered outside the embassy each day, hoping to gain entry to the US. In 1990 alone, two years before the day that I stood outside the embassy, 450,000 Indians had emigrated to the US. That hot July morning, I took my place in the lines that had begun to form early outside the embassy, people pouring in from all parts of northern India, even setting up a makeshift camp on the cement pavement outside the building. The wait was so long that it had spawned its own cottage industry: those with greater means had paid someone else to stand in their place, occupying their rightful spot a few minutes before it was their turn to enter the building.

After a wait of almost three hours in the hot sun, it was my turn to enter the building. The man behind the plastic partition at the counter looked fresh and unruffled, his blond hair slicked back and no half-moons of perspiration under his armpits. I had been warned by other students that the path to an American education was paved with visa hurdles and that consular officers, like the one before me, were the gatekeepers of the American dream. I offered a jaunty "Good morning," to which he simply looked up, met my gaze, and looked back down at the papers before him. I once again went through my mental checklist: I-20, check, vaccination records, check, admission letter, check, bank documents, check . . . the loud thump of the officer's stamp made me jump. He handed me a slip of paper but kept the passport.

"It will be ready to pick up in three days," he said. I looked down at the slip of paper where the red stamp said "approved." It was over. I had my F-1 student visa. I could now leave for America, one among the 439,000 students that year who had also waited in lines outside US embassies all over the world. I looked up to thank the officer, but he had already turned away, beckoning the next applicant to step forward.

SO WHAT HAD BROUGHT me to that stage in North Carolina that afternoon, standing before two hundred undergraduate students, was not my father's aspirations nor my own ambitions to come to America for a bigger and brighter educational future, but rather it was something far simpler and universal: love. That August day when I'd left India, I was leaving to follow Vikram, to follow what I believed was my romantic destiny. In the process, I became an accidental international student: I came to the US for love, but I ended up staying in spite of it. My student visa turned out to be my ticket to a gilded future: American campuses, whose glossy brochures promised colonnaded buildings, sprawling green lawns, and smiling faces with high ponytails and sparkling blue eyes, soaking up the sun while expanding their minds. These were the American McMonuments of Higher Education, and I was now headed to one myself.

2

Coke, Cookies, and Church Sales

"What can I get you to drink, ma'am?"

The flight attendant's question woke me up. She was holding out a large, shrink-wrapped brown disc while pointing to the drinks.

"Some Coke, please," I said. She emptied a whole scoop of ice into a small cup, pouring the fizzy Coke out of a large plastic bottle. I took a swig of it, letting the bubbles rush up to my nose, inhaling its sharp smell. It was the real thing, no imitation Campa Cola, the Indian version. I held the shrink-wrapped snack up to Vikram questioningly.

"Chocolate chip cookie," he said. I had never eaten a chocolate chip cookie, let alone one that was so large, four times the size of the Britannia tea biscuits I was used to in India.

We arrived in Raleigh on a bright, clear day. The sky outside the plane window was pure blue with puffs of white clouds, 8,500 miles from the gray, smog-laden skies of Delhi.

Vikram's friend Scott was to receive us at the airport. He was waiting for us in the arrival hall, a tall figure in a sweatshirt and baseball cap. "Hey, man." He clapped Vikram on the shoulder and reached to take the heavy carry-on from my hand.

"You must be Rajeeka," he said with a lopsided smile that

made his blue eyes crinkle. I nodded, feeling too tongue-tied to correct the pronunciation of my name. Scott was a doctoral student in the same department as Vikram and they had begun the program together, soon becoming friends. He was from Ohio, an area of the US that Vikram had described to me as the Midwest.

Scott drove a deep maroon pickup truck with "Subaru" emblazoned on its side in large letters. The truck had plenty of room in the back for the four large suitcases Vikram and I were carrying between us. The three of us squeezed into the front and were off to Scott's place where we were going to spend the next couple of nights while we looked for housing.

Scott eased the truck onto the highway and I held tight as he picked up speed, the other cars whizzing past but managing to stay in their lanes. The roads were wide and smooth, lined with tall pine trees. After about twenty minutes of driving, we passed a green sign that said RALEIGH, and we entered the city. We drove past shops, but the roads were oddly deserted. I didn't say anything for fear of appearing ignorant. Perhaps the whole city was on a vacation.

THE NEXT MORNING, Scott dropped Vikram and me off at the campus of North Carolina State University. I felt excited yet nervous. Everything these past few months—the tests, the applications, the shopping, and the visa—had led up to this day. But I had also arrived just two days before classes began for the fall semester, skipping all the orientations for new international students, and relying instead on Vikram as my guide for everything.

Our first destination was the Psychology Department, where I would be beginning work on my doctoral degree. I was their first and only Indian student, an anomaly amongst all the other Indian students on campus who were enrolled in the sciences, engineering, or mathematics. Daniels Hall, the building that housed the engineering department, had been nicknamed "Dinesh" Hall by the Indian students—most of them male—who filled its halls, Dinesh being a common Indian male name.

Vikram and I walked across a sprawling green patch to a tall, nondescript brick building called Poe Hall where the Psychology Department was located. It looked nothing like the historic, charming buildings of the many brochures I had pored over just months earlier. We took the elevator to the seventh floor to meet my advisor, Dr. John Bishop. His assistant, Wanda Smith, a Black woman with perfectly set curls, was seated outside his office and looked up at me over her glasses just as Dr. Bishop emerged from his office.

"Hey, Vikram, how are you doing? And you must be Rajeeka," he said, extending his hand. I shook his hand limply, wanting to correct his mispronunciation of my name but once again letting it go. One didn't correct one's teachers. Dr. Bishop wore khaki pants and a blue checked shirt that matched his light blue eyes. He ushered us into his office, every inch of which was stacked with papers and books. Here and there were objets d'art that were decidedly non-Western, probably gathered on his travels.

Vikram and Dr. Bishop already knew each other as Vikram had visited him several times over the past few months to check in on the status of my application. Now here I was, on campus and in my advisor's office for the first time.

Vikram and Dr. Bishop made small talk about the North

Carolina weather and the start of the school year, while I stayed silent, not knowing what to say. Eventually Dr. Bishop shuffled through the papers on his desk, pulling out a list of courses.

"Here's what you might want to sign up for this first semester," he said to me. "There are some regular classes and then some seminars."

I found his choice of words odd. How did I know what I might want to do, and did I even have a choice? He was my professor, and shouldn't he be the one telling me what I needed to do? I was used to my Indian professors issuing orders like military generals, not offering gentle suggestions for a proposed course of action. I didn't know how a seminar was different from an introductory graduate class. Courses, seminars, credits, tuition, teaching assistantship—it was all a blur and a lot to absorb. How was I going to understand all of this? But I felt too foolish to ask. Instead, I pretended I knew what was happening, just as I had pretended that I knew how to write a personal essay.

LATER THAT EVENING, we went out for dinner with Scott and his girlfriend, Amy. Next to Scott's tall frame, she was short and plump, with a peaches and cream complexion and very dark hair. I had never met her before, but she greeted me with a wide smile and quick hug.

Amici's was an Italian restaurant. It was dark and cozy inside, the walls lined with wainscoting and framed photos of the owner's family. There seemed to be a green-and-red theme with a tablecloth of green and white checks and red napkins. Unlike the dour male waiters at most Indian restaurants, our waitress was a cheery blond with a high-pitched voice. She set down large plastic tumblers of iced tea, which appeared to be more ice than tea. I politely declined but longed instead for a cup of hot tea. I had been drinking tea since the age of sixteen, and this was the first time that I hadn't had any for two days at a stretch.

We ordered pizza and when it arrived, it was the largest thing I had ever seen. The waitress deftly sliced it using a sharp, circular blade. But there wasn't anything else to go with the pizza.

"May I have some ketchup, please?" I asked. The waitress looked at me in surprise as if I had made an unusual request.

"Let me see what I can do," she said. Meanwhile Vikram nudged me and whispered, "They don't eat ketchup with their pizza here."

I took a bite of the pizza, the soft mozzarella mingling with the rich and tart tomato sauce. The only pizzas I had eaten were at Delhi's famous Nirula's chain of restaurants, where the burgers and what passed for pizza had a decidedly Indian touch. But my friends and I had loved the food, putting up with the crowded buses to travel to the Nirula's in Connaught Place, the heart of the city. My friend Rupal and I would save money so that we could visit the Nirula's salad bar once a month. A day or so before our visit, we would embark on a fast of sorts by consuming less of the horrible hostel food, all the while building our appetites in anticipation of the array of delicious foods at the salad bar. Once there, we disregarded anything that remotely resembled a raw vegetable and instead headed straight for the creamy Russian salad and dishes with mayonnaise. And there was always ketchup and Nirula's special sharp mustard available, and lots of it.

The check arrived, and I watched as both Vikram and Scott pulled out their wallets. There was no snatching of the bill from the billfold, no good-natured bickering over who would pay—a drama that typically unfolded when Indians dined out together, each vying to be more generous than the other. But here it was clean and clinical: Vikram and Scott both perused the bill and agreed that we had all eaten an equal amount and so it made the most sense to split it halfway. No drama, and no one was the poorer for it.

But I was still confused about the ketchup episode.

"Why was everyone so surprised when I asked for ketchup with the pizza?" I asked Vikram, once we were by ourselves later that night.

"Because pizza is originally from Italy, where they don't eat it with ketchup, and because it already has a base of tomato sauce."

I had no idea.

THE NEXT MORNING Vikram and I began our search for an apartment. It had to be close to campus and on the bus line. We drove up and down Avent Ferry Road and Gorman Street, where every apartment complex looked the same as the next. We finally settled on one called Glendale Village, its streets named after trees: Elm, Maple, Juniper. But despite the tall trees and green landscaping, the apartment buildings themselves were anything but charming. The facade of the apartments was a nondescript brick with a gray trim, with gray wooden staircases separating the various blocks of apartments. But no one back home in India would know this. The address on my letters—230 Juniper Drive —would likely conjure up the image of clean, wholesome America and verdant enclaves of refined, communal living. It looked like the sort of place I had seen in the numerous photographs that my father's brother, Uncle Satish, would send home to India from Virginia, showing him beaming proudly as he leaned against a shiny car parked outside a complex exactly such as this.

Scott drove us up to the Glendale Village rental office in his truck. A middle-aged woman squeezed into a tight, bright pink dress and with big, coiffed blond hair looked up as the chime on the door alerted her to our arrival. Her heavily mascaraed eyes took in Scott and then settled on Vikram and me.

"Hi, honeys," she said, but it came out more as a long drawn-out "H-a-a-a hurneys." "I'm Pam," she added, in what I was already beginning to identify as an accent I had never heard in most of the Hollywood films I had seen back in India.

Her heavily ringed hands waved us into the chairs placed across from her desk. "What can I do for you?" she asked in an exaggerated and loud manner, as if we were deaf.

"Do you have any apartments available?" Vikram asked.

"Oh, sure, hur-ney. We have a two-bedroom that's popular with the college kids. But you'll have to pay a deposit, you know."

I could sense Scott shifting uncomfortably in his chair, but he was too polite to say anything.

I felt suddenly small, as if we had nothing—even though we had our checkbooks ready to write out a deposit and one month's rent. But we were thousands of miles away from home, with no family here to help us, no savings, no safety net, and here was this woman talking down to us in this way. What could she possibly know about where we came from? She did not know that Vikram came from an influential family in India where everyone was either a lawyer, a doctor, or a senior civil servant, or that my mother was a professor of English literature and could probably teach Pam a thing or two about English. Or that both Vikram and I had been to two of India's best private schools and top undergraduate colleges. But she did not or would not ever know any of this. All she could see was our brown skin, and all she could hear were our strange accents.

Pam drove us over to show us the vacant apartment. It was boxy and all sharp angles. The carpet was an insipid buff color but reasonably clean. I had never lived with wall-to-wall carpeting before and wondered how we would keep it clean without the daily ritual of sweeping and mopping that occurred in homes in India. There was a living-cum-dining room, a kitchen, two bedrooms, and one bathroom. Nothing more, nothing less. Just enough.

"We'll take it," we said, not knowing what other options we had. Classes began in exactly two days, and we needed a place to live. I wrote out the check for the deposit and the rent: $1,300, which was equal to 58,500 rupees. My hands shook as I handed Pam the check. That small, rectangular piece of paper was the equivalent of a handsome monthly salary in India. It was half the price of a compact Maruti car in India and could buy a round-trip air ticket to America. I didn't think of it that way then, but it was a small part of the billions that international students like me contributed to the US economy in 1992.

WE NOW HAD a place to live, but there was the sticky issue of how to break the news to our families. Telling them that we were living in the same apartment, under the same roof, was out of the question. Yet living separately made no sense as we were engaged to be married soon, and there was no way we could afford two separate rents when instead we could be saving money toward a car and our annual visits to India. We could barely afford the rent for the two-bedroom in Glendale Village. The ideal solution was to bring in someone to share our apartment, preferably a woman who would also provide the perfect foil of being my roommate.

Vikram made flyers which he then stapled to bulletin boards all over campus. Nehir Yildiz responded to our ad. She was from Turkey, a country that I knew nothing about. She seemed mild enough and was unfazed at the idea of rooming with an Indian couple. She was probably a bit older than Vikram and me, with a stocky build, a broad face, and a head of thick spiral curls. Her small eyes squinted through her glasses, giving her a perpetually puzzled look. Like us, she brought with her two suitcases when she moved in. But unlike us, she seemed to have more money and had already acquired a car for herself—a flaming orange Nissan—that she drove around Raleigh to the classes that she was taking to learn English. She had just learned driving, and this was evident in the way she drove, missing turns and instead driving over sidewalks. The only food she ate was pasta heaped on her plate, slathered with a plain tomato sauce and tossed with ground meat.

Our families were told that I had rented an apartment with a female roommate and that the apartment had an attached studio of sorts that served as Vikram's living quarters. We managed to get a split phone line from AT&T that provided two seemingly separate phone numbers, one for Vikram and one for me. All this seemed to provide the requisite physical distance in our living arrangement, while also appearing to be a fiscally prudent decision. But Vikram's parents and my mother knew that we were living together, and we knew that they knew. We made a silent pact in which no one questioned or even mentioned the arrangement. As with most things Indian, what mattered most was the veneer of respectability.

Our apartment began to slowly come together. Even though Vikram and I had very little money, I began to create a home for us with the odds and ends we collected at yard sales. At first, I was amazed that people would sell their used stuff, and even more surprised that people would buy it. But we couldn't afford much better and began to visit neighborhood church sales through which other international students like us had furnished their places. Our biggest purchase was a hideous but sturdy sofa set of clunky, dark wood with large cushions of green-and-red printed upholstery. For a side table I repurposed a large box and draped it with some printed fabric and on it placed a small arrangement of artificial flowers, also bought at the yard sale.

Scott and Amy donated a wicker and glass dining table with dangerously rickety chairs. I bought cheap pots and pans for the kitchen from discount stores like Big Lots. Photographs of our friends and family began to appear on our walls in frames bought at the dollar store. In between all that we were acquiring was the Indian bric-a-brac we had carried with us—the soapstone coasters with paintings of miniature elephants, the Rajasthani wall hanging with the classic mirror-work, and enameled brass vases. Our home was shaping up to be part-American and part-Indian, or at least whatever bits of India we could bring in our suitcases.

3

You Can't Go Home Again

Coming to America was not the first time I had traveled for school. I was twelve when I first left home. It was 1983, and even though my parents were divorced by then, they put up a rare united front and came together to drop me off at my boarding school in the hills. We stayed in a small hotel in Kasauli, a hill station that overlooked the Lawrence School Sanawar. The day of the school visit, my mother wore a smart navy-blue pantsuit and large sunglasses, the perfect vision of a modern Indian woman who had moved beyond her traditional saris and escaped an unhappy marriage. She had been to the same school as a child and wasn't sure who she would run into. My father had reservations about sending me away to a school so far from home, where we got to see our parents only a few times a year and where the only form of communication was old-fashioned mail.

When the time came for them to say goodbye, I didn't cry, even though it would be months before I would see my mother. I was excited and eager to join the girls and boys in their neat gray-and-red uniforms. All I could think of that day were the St. Clare's and Malory Towers book series by Enid Blyton that I had read growing up, which were set in boarding schools just like

- peg of whiskey
- when 6 andhi goto S. Africa?

Sanawar, with its old British buildings and cold, damp hallways. I would now get to be a part of something just like that, except that the Cornish seaside of Malory Towers was replaced by a hillside in the foothills of the Himalayas.

I was not the first in my family to leave home to study. My father's family has a history of moving in pursuit of an education. The first one to leave Indian shores was my paternal grandfather, D. P. Bhandari, who sailed to England in 1932 to study law at Cambridge. He had taken the competitive Indian Civil Services examination (ICS) that year on a whim, never expecting to be selected. But when he not only passed but was at the top of the list of successful ICS candidates, he was sent to England for a year. It was the period before the partition of India and Pakistan and it was the proper thing in those days for young, refined Indians who aspired to be just like the British to go overseas and be educated in British ways, returning to India as *pukka sahibs* who would lead India into its future, much as Gandhi had done when he had gone to London in 1888 to study as a lawyer.

My grandfather was very much in the elite ICS mold. After his return to India, he never fully shed the British mannerisms he acquired during his year abroad and would sit down to breakfast each day after a bath, dressed in pinstripes, suspenders, and a bow tie, his hair slicked back with pomade—the perfect image of a barrister. He also developed a fondness for marmalade and salad cream, both of which were always stocked in the fridge at my grandparents' house even during hard times when other staples were in short supply. He would end his day on a tufted leather sofa, tuned into the BBC on a large classic Phillips radio, while enjoying a peg of whiskey with tepid water, ideally with one of his sons. Yet he spoke to my grandmother and his children most often in Punjabi, whose guttural tone was jarring against his British-inspired refined ways.

By the time I was growing up, my grandfather never spoke much about his time in the ICS, leading to speculation on my mother's side of the family as to whether my paternal grandfather had actually attended Cambridge, or whether it was a convenient fabrication kept alive by my father, the oldest son. We were never quite sure. But many years later, much after my grandfather had passed away and the Bhandari family had dispersed all over the world—from New Zealand to the US, and everywhere in between—I found hard evidence of my grandfather's sojourn: his original Cambridge diploma pasted on the wall of my father's apartment in Delhi.

My grandmother, too, experimented with a foreign degree. While she never actually traveled abroad to study—it was rare for Indian women to do so in the 1930s—she was the first woman to get a degree from the University of Jammu, in the northern Indian state of Jammu and Kashmir, while also obtaining a correspondence certificate in fine arts from the Royal College of Art in London. So, almost a century ago, my grandmother was already engaging in what we today call distance learning. She never did much with her degrees, but they helped secure a good marriage for her which, in those days, was the only reason for a girl to be educated. Many years later she would fulfill her quest for knowledge by keeping up with the monthly *Reader's Digest* magazines that my grandfather subscribed to, reading late into the night under the light of a red table lamp after everyone had gone to bed and all the household chores had been completed.

When it came to the next generation—my father and his six siblings—three ventured abroad to study. In a newly independent India, ambitious students continued to look westwards but were now setting their sights beyond England. America, an Anglophone country with over four thousand colleges and universities, and a nation where hard work was rewarded with success, seemed like a natural destination. The first to leave India was Uncle Satish, the rising intellectual star of the Bhandari family. Unlike my father, he was neither a dashing sportsman nor a ladies' man. But he was smart enough to get admission into the nuclear physics program at Carnegie Mellon University in 1975. He was part of the second wave of Indians who arrived in the US in large numbers but were different from the Indian immigrants of the nineteenth century who had helped build America's agriculture and railroad industries. In the 1960s, the doors of the nation had been reopened to the world's best and brightest. In the decades that followed, thousands arrived in the US, filling science and engineering departments with their aspirations and their determination to live the American dream.

I was Uncle Satish's favorite niece and awaited his annual visits back to India eagerly, for he would always come home laden with gifts. When he opened his suitcases, everything in them smelled fresh and crisp, with what I would later identify as the fragrance of laundry detergent and dryer sheets. It was a clean, first-world smell of opportunity and optimism that washed away the grittiness of Delhi. The first gift Uncle Satish got me was a pinafore dress, then a black sweater with polka dots which I wore throughout my college days in Delhi, and then a collection of mugs announcing the greatness of all things American—the Statue of Liberty, the New York City skyline, and even one with the mascot of his alma mater, Carnegie Mellon University. For his siblings, he brought back Levi's jeans,

sweatshirts, and sneakers. For my grandmother, it was her favorite dusters which she wore at home, over the years replacing
the impractical sari with the comfortable gowns with their utilitarian pockets. She also always asked my uncle to bring back
almonds. This always surprised me since almonds were plentiful
in India, until I learned later how expensive they were. Just because they were readily available didn't make them easily acces-
sible.

As was de rigueur for young Indian students like him, my
uncle probably dated American women but eventually acquired
a doe-eyed, young Indian bride. On one of his trips home, the
couple was introduced, the match approved, the wedding hastily
arranged, and he brought his bride back with him to the US.
They went on to be the prototype of successful Indian immigrants—the model minority—with large suburban homes, manicured lawns, white picket fences, and gleaming cars. Their two
boys attended exemplary public schools in New Jersey and
Maryland, before heading to top US universities.

But my father, the oldest of seven, never studied abroad, and
perhaps because he didn't, it became a lifelong preoccupation
for him. He always viewed it as a lost opportunity, often comparing himself with his classmates at St. Stephens College, Delhi's
elite Jesuit institution, many of whom were the sons of successful
diplomats and went on to an Oxbridge education befitting their
heritage. My father, on the other hand, completed his education
at the University of Delhi, choosing to abandon professional
cricket and instead pursuing a career in journalism. He eventually
traveled abroad for his work, seeing the whole world and sating
his wanderlust, but the hallowed portals of a British or American
university remained beyond his reach. So he ended up dreaming

that I would complete my undergraduate education in India and then go abroad to study in the US, following in the footsteps of his brothers who had managed to "get away."

ON MY MOTHER'S side, too, the quest for a high-quality education and learning began very early. My mother had left home when she was just six to join one of India's most prestigious boarding schools, the Lawrence School, Sanawar—the boarding school that I too ultimately attended.

How my mother, the youngest of three children, born into a working-class, albeit upwardly mobile Punjabi family, came to attend an elite British-era school is the stuff of legend. Her father, my maternal grandfather, was ambitious for himself and his children. After his training with the British Roadways in England, he scaled the ladder of the Delhi Transport Corporation from the lowly rung of a clerical officer to become the general manager of the fleet of buses that kept the large city of Delhi moving.

He wanted more for his children, and the story goes that he took my mother and my uncle (who was just a year older) to an entrance exam for India's highly selective private schools, most of which were residential schools tucked away in serene hill stations. Those who passed the exam with high grades but were unable to afford such an education were offered scholarships— the schools' attempt at infusing diversity into their student body.

It turned out that both my mother and her brother did well, but the Lawrence School asked my grandfather to choose, since it wouldn't be fair to offer two scholarships to the same family. You would think my grandfather's choice would be obvious, but he instead chose to send my mother to Sanawar. It was a move that even in today's India would be considered radical and progressive, and far more so in 1953, a time when gender discrimination in India ran deep and boys were valued more than girls. Boys were trained for their intellectual potential, while girls were groomed to be beautiful and domesticated. Rudyard Kipling, the chronicler of the British Raj in India, wrote famously in his 1901 novel, *Kim*, that its eponymous hero should be "sent to Sanawar to make a man of him." But my grandfather defied convention and sent his daughter there instead. With that one momentous decision, my grandfather forever altered my mother's destiny, helping her become the woman and person she would eventually be.

That is how a young girl from a simple family ended up at a fancy school in the Himalayan foothills, where morning tea was called *Chotta Hazari*—the term evoking the British era when servants carried out the morning tea ritual—and where the students lined up to the call of the bugle. But it was a choice for which my grandmother never forgave my grandfather, for her son was the apple of her eye.

What must it have been like for my mother to leave home at such a young age? To be surrounded by strangers and all things unfamiliar on a hilltop, miles away from home? What must it have felt like to be one of the few scholarship students among kids from affluent families? None of this could have been easy. But my mother firmly believes that her time at Sanawar provided her with the education and sheer expansion of mind and thinking she needed to chart a course in her life that was radically different from anything the Anand family had ever known. It was the independence acquired at such a young age that gave her the gumption at the age of twenty-seven, with a five-year-old child and living in a small Indian town with a provincial mentality, to leave an unhappy marriage and file for divorce. This was an act that was unheard of in the mid-1970s in India, and something that would remain an albatross around her neck. Despite her protestations over the years, everyone continued to say that "her husband had left her." For a woman to be the one to leave her man was simply unthinkable.

It was this early schooling that also provided the foundation for my mother to push on and acquire a master's degree while her marriage was falling apart, to recognize that an education and job would be her ticket to freedom, and to ultimately go on to also obtain a PhD. Her implicit belief in the value of a quality education allowed her to eventually send me far away from her, from the deep interiors of the central Indian city of Bhopal that lacked good schools to the foothills of the Himalayan mountains, to the same boarding school that she had attended. I left home at the age of twelve, never to look back. After my schooling in Sanawar, it was three years of college in Delhi, and then the US.

But as I thought about the stories of my family and those who had come before me, I realized that I was not alone in my journey to America as an international student. I was carrying with me the educational dreams of many generations of the Bhandari and Anand families.

4

Classroom Lessons

"**T**his is the computer lab," Sarah said, opening a door. I followed her in. I was Sarah Branford's teaching assistant and had been assigned to two classes, hers and Dr. Broussard's. I suppose she didn't know what to make of me and was inwardly wondering why she had been assigned the only international TA in the whole department. She was a small-built woman, pale, with a shock of dark and wavy hair. When she smiled, which she did often, her braces seemed to take up her entire face. It was the first time I was meeting an adult with braces. I had gone through the childhood ordeal of wearing braces, but I thought they were only for children and that most adults would be too self-conscious and vain to sport them. But I was learning that, as with many things in America, it was never too late to do something different, to change course—whether it was correcting the teeth you were born with or deciding that you wanted to be a professional scuba diver instead of a statistician. America, I was discovering, was a land of reinvention.

The computer lab was a long room with a low perforated ceiling filled with row after row of white machines with heads bent over them. It was unlike anything I had ever seen before. At the front of the lab sat a man, reclining deep in his chair, chewing gum and surveying the anxious students clicking away at the keyboards. He was older and portly, his sparse hair pulled back in a ponytail. Sarah and I walked over to him.

"Chad, this is our new grad student, Rajika," Sarah said, and then after a pause, "from India," which got Chad's attention. Sarah then added what felt like a death sentence, "She doesn't know much about computers and needs help."

"Really? Wow, well, okay then . . . let's see what we can do," said Chad, getting up and stretching lazily before walking around his desk. I felt a telltale flush rising from my neck and didn't know where to look. I hoped none of the other students in the lab had heard our conversation. The truth was that I knew nothing about using a computer or even about typing. And yet here I was, in a country and a culture where I was supposed to know how to type on a QWERTY keyboard, fingers flying over the keys with eyes trained on the screen, whipping out page after page of typed assignments.

The first time I'd seen a computer had been in 1986. I was in the tenth grade when my boarding school acquired three precious computers and placed them in a small, sealed-off room to protect them from dust. Some of the older boys were invited in to try out these new machines and take classes, but the machines were not to be used by just anybody, for they were expensive and had been procured with difficulty. Using them was a rare privilege that appeared to be reserved for boys. What happened in that lab seemed to be top secret.

By the time I landed in Delhi for college two years later, I still didn't know anything about computers. I thought I had little need to learn how to use one—after all, small typists' kiosks all over the city were now offering "word processing services."

But there was something more crisp and professional about print than handwriting, and I began to wonder whether my assignments would look nicer if they were typed up. With my mother's help, I acquired a used electronic typewriter in a sleek red case with a handle which ostensibly made the heavy contraption portable. Then came the challenge of typing. I couldn't imagine sitting for hours in a sweaty, smelly typing shop, learning typing from a betel nut–chewing man with grubby fingers who would likely be looking down my blouse on the pretext of teaching me typing. So I struggled alone in my hostel room, one finger at a time, trying to make some sense and rhythm out of the keys, willing my hands to fly faster and faster.

I could have asked my father for help. Even though none of my friends in India knew how to type, let alone use a computer, my father could type very fast. For a journalist, it was a mandatory skill. As a child, before my parents divorced and he moved out, I'd often awakened to the staccato of typewriter keys as he typed off his articles. His typewriter was an old green Olivetti, and his office always smelled of fresh type and carbon paper, which he used in great excess as he believed in keeping a copy of everything. So I could have asked my father for advice. But he lived 1,400 kilometers away in Bombay, and in his characteristic fashion he would have asked too many probing questions: What was I doing with a typewriter? How did I get it? How much did I pay for it? Did I pay too much? Why did I think I needed to type my college papers?

Not having to do your own typing was also a status symbol in India, a sign of having arrived, where one would have a private office with an air conditioner and a sleek computer which would never be used but would be cleaned and dusted daily like a revered idol. Prim, docile secretaries would be given dictation and would scurry off to convert their shorthand into long-winded, stuffy letters with words such as "herewith," "therefore," "aforementioned," and "doing the needful," which was often the intent of such dispatches—to get the recipient to do his or her needful duty. Here, in America, I noticed that my advisor, Dr. Bishop, seldom asked Wanda to do anything for him, let alone type for him. In fact, he treated her with a deferential air, apologizing in advance of any request he made of her.

In India, my efforts at college to deliver crisp, printed papers were dismissed equally crisply by my psychology teachers. Dr. Agarwal, herself a US-educated professor, stared down her long nose and remarked, "Lot of trouble you went through, but not necessary," before flinging my paper on top of the other stack of handwritten papers.

But typing on a computer was a necessity in the US. Why had no one warned me about this? Why had the counselor at the United States Educational Foundation in Delhi not said anything about this fundamental requirement? Everyone had talked about admissions tests, personal essays, choosing the right university, and so on and so forth, but no one had mentioned this one essential skill needed to succeed in an American classroom—that you had to know how to type and use a computer. It was something that was simply assumed, and yet in the months to come it became my biggest hurdle.

Chad led me over to a row of boxy machines that were much smaller than the other computers. "If you don't know much about computers, then this Mac is your best bet, right?" he said, looking at me for affirmation. But I remained silent because I didn't know what a Mac was.

I pulled out the chair and sat down before the dark screen. The Mac had an odd shape, almost toylike in its size and simplicity. Chad turned it on and then walked away.

The Mac and I were on our own. Soon the screen lit up and, to my surprise, a smiley face appeared. I had expected scrolling lines of neon text and digits. This might just be simple enough, I thought, pulling back my shoulders and settling into my first self-taught computer tutorial.

LATER THAT AFTERNOON, it was time for my first graduate class: Community Psychology taught by Dr. Bishop. The class was called a seminar, and I wasn't sure what that meant. There were eight of us clustered around the table, all of whom had just begun the graduate program. There was a sense of anticipation in the air, lined yellow notepads neatly laid out and pens poised. How I had always longed for those yellow legal pads. Vikram had brought back a few on his first visit back from the US, and all his long letters were written to me on those pages. I would run my hand over them, their smooth texture an invitation to write, a fresh smell emanating from them that I was beginning to associate with everything American. And now here I was, in this American classroom, with my American classmates, and with my very own American pad before me.

Dr. Bishop entered the room and nodded at us with an awkward smile. He took a seat at the head of the table and then asked each of us to introduce ourselves. I was not used to this business of talking about oneself. Writing the personal essay had been hard enough, but here it was again, this idea of holding forth about oneself in a detached and objective manner, to "get on one's soapbox," as Americans called it. I was having to speak up in ways I never had to before.

In India, our teachers would take attendance, checking off our names on a list. Beyond that, they rarely asked why we were there or what we hoped to get out of the class. We were expected to be quiet, especially if we were women. To ask questions would be to disrupt the flow of the class and to question the authority of the teacher.

We all began to go around the table, one by one, introducing ourselves.

"Hi all, I'm Daniel Helms. I used to run my own company in client relations but thought it would be good to go back to school to expand my learning. Really great to be here with all of you!" Daniel was skinny, with longish wavy hair, and a toothy smile.

"Good morning, I'm Anne Kessler and I'm delighted to be here. I used to work with Microsoft but wanted to go back to school to get a PhD."

"Hey all, I'm Anna Jensen and I'm so excited to be here!"

When it was my turn, I felt stumped. How to summarize my college years, or why I was here? Should I tell the truth that I had simply followed Vikram? But that didn't sound as weighty as the aspirations of those sitting around the table. My classmates were brimming with a sense of purpose that I didn't share.

While on the surface my chosen path seemed clear-cut and deliberate, on the inside it was anything but, for I had never sat down and mapped how each step would ultimately lead to a desired outcome. Simply put, I was toeing the line that many Indians had before me: we went through our education in one shot —high school, college, and postgraduate study—with no delay or departure from this linear formula. Going to college was just something everyone did, to improve either their job or marriage prospects. This was probably why India had an overabundance of aimless and uninspired college graduates, many of them underemployed at Western-style fast-food chains where their English-speaking skills came in handy.

For Indian students, there was no notion of taking a summer off to go abroad, to do an internship, or to backpack through Europe in a modern version of the eighteenth-century Grand Tour where, sitting atop an isolated hilltop, one would perhaps discover one's true calling. Had I allowed myself the self-indulgence and luxury of "discovering myself," I might have become an interior designer, an artist, or a journalist, wishful ideas that I'd sacrificed at the altar of practicality and the comfortable predictability of a viable, solid career. Self-exploration is not something that we Indians do, or at least not until we have a few gray hairs and decades' worth of experience, when the process of introspection is more about the regret for the road not taken rather than the excitement of the journey ahead.

Now, with all eyes on me, I felt the pressure to speak, lest my silence be mistaken for stupidity. It was bad enough that I was the only one who looked different, had a strange name, and sounded different, even to my own ears. But all I could muster for now was, "Hello, I'm Rajika Bhandari, and I'm from India." For now, my apparent foreignness defined me and confined me.

ONE THING WAS becoming clear to me: American classrooms were nothing like those in India. The differences began with something as basic as how each of us sat in class. It amazed me that American students chomped and slurped their way through classes and occasionally propped their feet up on the furniture. Then there was the custom of referring to professors by their first names. Such casualness seemed to somehow diminish the importance of the education we were there to receive.

American professors taught us as if we were coconspirators, allies in the pursuit of knowledge: they advised, guided, and consulted. My Indian professors, by contrast, had commanded us from the front of the classroom, frowning and glowering, hell-bent on making us master the basics and, in the process, squelching our love for the subject at hand. American students pondered, researched, and critiqued, whereas Indian students like me were used to learning by rote, committing everything to memory but very little to true comprehension. During my college days in Delhi, I had become used to an academic calendar of seven months of lackluster performance in class, followed by three months of intense cramming ahead of the final, high-stakes exam. In the last few weeks leading up to the exam, the women's hostel would be abuzz all night, as we paced up and down, notebooks in hand, fueled by endless cups of coffee and the odious smoke emitted from mosquito coils as we memorized all the facts and figures that we were supposed to have imbibed over the course of the year.

Yet this approach must have some merits because Indian students—and other Asian students who had been taught at home in similar ways—were widely regarded as being brainy and smart in American institutions. Many succeeded in the classroom, then went on to fuel science and innovation in the US. What accounted for our success, when it was so clear that how and what we were taught was so different from what we encountered in the US? Were we indeed simply smarter than other students, or were our deeply ingrained habits of diligence and hard work, honed over years of exposure to more traditional education, the ultimate keys to our future success?

Now at NC State, instead of an overreliance on a single, annual, high-stakes exam, there were pop quizzes in addition to end-of-term exams, which meant that we were assessed frequently on what we were learning. This forced me to learn in a whole new way. For starters, I had to gather and read large amounts of material. Through trial and error, I taught myself to use the library catalog and databases to do a literature search. I was too embarrassed to ask my classmates about the difference between an abstract and a full research paper, or about the conventions of constructing a compelling literature review. Years later, while teaching at a university in New York, I would have the opportunity to witness how many international students—particularly those who struggle with English—were suspected of plagiarism, when in fact what students were encountering was a complex mix of language, culture, and ignorance about the process of researching and synthesizing information. As an international student at NCSU, I too did not fully understand plagiarism and what it meant to paraphrase or quote information. It was assumed that I would know all of this before beginning my graduate program. Again, I found myself wondering whether we international students were really prepared to succeed in American classrooms.

THE TOPIC FOR Sarah's first class on Introduction to Psychology for which I was a TA was perceptions of race and color. I wondered whether it was deliberate or an uncanny coincidence that both she and Dr. Broussard had chosen to begin their first class with the same topic. But this similarity aside, there were many differences between the two teachers. The most obvious difference: he was a tall, large-built Black man, and she was a diminutive white woman. And unlike Dr. Broussard, who treated the front of the lecture hall as a stage, pacing up and down while lecturing in his booming voice, Sarah sought the protective armor of the lectern, delivering her lecture methodically while using the mike to amplify her nasal voice.

When Sarah's lecture was over, I went and stood next to her, handing out assignments to the students as they filed out. One of the students strode up to Sarah, looking visibly upset. He was a Black man, older than the other students (probably about forty-five), and he wore a long trench coat and stylish hat.

"Ms. Branford, I respect you and what you're teaching, but a lot of this is nonsense and doesn't in any way reflect what's going on with us African Americans in this country."

Sarah was taken aback and hastily gathered up her papers from the lectern. She nodded vigorously at the man.

"I'm happy to hear your thoughts, but I—"

"I just don't understand how you can teach this stuff," he said, cutting Sarah off mid-sentence. He was clearly agitated, and I wondered whether I could defuse the situation.

I stepped up closer to him and said in the kindest voice possible.

"I know exactly how you must feel as an outsider in this country. I myself just arrived here some weeks ago from India."

I thought my reassuring tone would make him calm down, to see that he wasn't the only one who looked different and felt alienated. Instead he turned to me, his eyes widening and his mouth opening and closing silently. Sarah paled even further, if that was possible, and quickly ushered me out of the room, looking over her shoulder to mouth an apology to the man. He just shook his head, a look of disbelief and disgust on his face, and walked away.

What had I done wrong? He seemed different from most Americans, in much the way that I felt and looked different. Up until then, my interaction with Black Americans had been limited to the receptionists, librarians, and cafeteria workers who staffed the university. The only other Black professors I knew were Daniel Williams, who was beginning to embrace his West African heritage, occasionally sporting a kufi cap and outfits made from kente cloth; and Dr. Broussard, who was from New Orleans and seemed more French than African.

Most of the Indian students I knew at NC State shunned Black students, calling them "*kallus*," a pejorative term that literally meant "blackie," and regarding them with a mixture of fascination and horror. Equating dark skin with all things evil ran deep within the Indian community. Shortly before I had left for the US, my grandfather had asked me with genuine curiosity: Is it true that there are many habshis in America? *Habshi*, as African and Abyssinian slaves were known in pre-British India, or a word that evoked the dark-skinned villains of Indian classics like the Ramayana and Mahabharata.

"No, Nana, how can you say that!" I chided him. But now when I saw that most Indian students had the same attitudes when studying alongside Black Americans, I had to wonder whether we were fundamentally racist, looking down on all individuals—Indian or American—who were dark-skinned.

film *Mississippi Masala* had been released just six months before I had arrived in the US and had created a controversy because its central plot was one of the most taboo subjects within the Indian community in the US—a liaison between a Black man and an Indian woman. I had to wonder whether America to us meant an all-white country, while instead we had to contend with Black people, Latinos, and others who somehow tarnished the gilded America that we all sought.

I was discovering that understanding race relations in America and India's complex history with skin color were lessons that were much harder than figuring out how to use a Mac.

5

It Takes a Village

I boarded the Wolf Line bus on campus and settled into my seat as the bus slowly made its way to Gorman Street. It began to empty out as it approached Avent Ferry Road with its cluster of condominiums, and soon it was just the group of Indian students huddled together at the back of the bus, a few American students, and I. The Indian students chatted loudly, but I couldn't understand what they were saying. All I could discern was that they were speaking a South Indian language, probably Tamil. This was an unfortunate legacy of India's British colonial history, where the only language that united a country of 1.4 billion people was English. Here in North Carolina, too, the only language that my Indian friends and I had in common was English. Soon we Indians were the only ones left on the bus, and we all got off at Glendale Village, the last stop on the route.

Five months had passed since I had arrived in Raleigh, and I was discovering that, far from being a quaint rural haven as its name suggested, Glendale Village was a veritable ghetto of international students. The foreign students—most of them Indian—were crowded into small apartments or townhouses, sharing rooms, food, and toilet paper. Should one ever run out of something, it was easy enough to borrow it. Perhaps it was my imagination, but the smell of spices wafted through the subdivision as we Indian students experimented with replicating Indian dishes in our American kitchens. By then, I had watched enough episodes of *The Simpsons* with the Apu Nahasapeemapetilon character to know how most Americans viewed Indians, and I longed to dispel the stereotype that we all reeked of curry and greasy hair oil.

And yet, how could I ignore the groups of young *desi* men at the back of the Wolf Line bus, smelling of an odd blend of hair oil, incense, and rancid sweat? They had discovered Coke and McDonald's, but not the universal American habit of using deodorant daily. I glanced around me and could sense the American students in the bus cringing and almost holding their breath. I wanted to announce to everyone in the bus: "Yes, we smell of spices, but it's also because your kitchens and homes don't have any ventilation!" Who in their right minds would build apartments with no windows in the kitchens and bathrooms, yet install wall-to-wall carpeting that absorbed and retained all the aroma from the spices? I felt the urge to stand up for my heritage like the proud model minority I was supposed to be.

But to take on defending a whole subcontinent was too much for me. Instead, I learned to make my own small adjustments so that I would fit in to my new American surroundings. Each time I cooked, I changed out of my "outside" clothes into casual clothes and kept my long hair tied up so that it wouldn't absorb the vapors from my cooking. And then I changed back into my proper clothes when going out.

At Glendale Village, I was surrounded by other students like myself. In the apartment above Vikram, Nehir, and me lived Ashish and Ravi. Both were newly arrived graduate students

p. 31

from India, both (of course) studying engineering. Ashish ambled around in shorts, a short-sleeved shirt, and Bata flip-flops, relaxing with a cigarette every now and then. I heard Ravi before I ever saw him. His bedroom was right above mine and I could hear him on the phone for hours on end, his high-pitched voice drifting out of his open window. He apparently had a girlfriend back in Bombay, hence the long phone chats.

We were in America, and yet Glendale Village felt like a different world, where the occasional American was viewed as an oddity. One Friday evening, as several of us were gathered for a potluck dinner, there was a knock at the door. Our host, Mahesh, went to the door and announced upon returning, "It's one of those foreigners." One of his American neighbors, Carl, had stopped by to ask Mahesh if he could use his parking spot for a visiting friend's car. Gathered there that evening, we were the foreigners, the "nonresident aliens," to be precise, and yet here was Carl, regarded by Mahesh as a foreigner in his own backyard.

On a deeper level, however, for most Indians foreignness had more to do with whiteness than with being a stranger or an outsider. Back in India, any white-skinned woman—American, British, Russian—was considered a foreigner. Before arriving in Raleigh, the only "foreign," or white, young women I had ever met were the few exchange students who came to my boarding school for a term or two. Some were American, while others were Swiss or German, I couldn't be certain. To me, they all seemed the same, for they were all tall, blond, and blue-eyed. And they all seemed to be unconcerned about being seen in the nude. When it was time to change out of our uniforms into our nightclothes, we Indian girls had figured out the tricky maneu-

[handwritten margin notes: "or not. that dark / skin ⊖ a matter / or odd girls / to be sent to Indian bigschool" — with "56"]

ver of removing one sleeve and then the other, deftly removing the bra without baring an inch of skin—all this in an overcrowded dormitory of almost a hundred girls. But the foreign girls would simply sit on their beds and remove their shirts with a nonchalance that suggested that undressing before their own kind was the most natural thing in the world. Their beds were to the front of the dormitory, so all I could see was the milky-white bare skin of their backs.

ANNA JENSEN WAS one of a handful of intrepid Americans who ventured to live amongst so many international students in Glendale Village. She was the all-American girl of glossy magazines, tall, squeaky-clean, and with the quintessential high ponytail tucked into a baseball cap. She was so blond that her eyelashes sparkled golden when they caught the sunlight. She was from Kansas, and I learned that her Germanic heritage explained her unusual height and broad bone structure.

Anna and I began the graduate program in psychology at the same time. We often sat next to each other in class, and I was beginning to realize that, just as there were so many accents of English in India, there were many different American English accents. Anna's accent was different from the Southern drawl, her "eggs" sounded like "Ehggs," and "been" came out as a "ben."

Anna lived across from me in Glendale Village. The first time she invited me over to her apartment, I was taken aback. I looked around, expecting another roommate to materialize— for her apartment to provide some evidence that she was a struggling graduate student just like me—but instead I learned that she lived in the one-bedroom apartment all by herself, paying a rent of $625 a month. Our teaching assistantships paid only $700 a month, and all the international graduate students I knew were living squeezed into one- or two-bedroom apartments; for us, an apartment of one's own was an unimaginable luxury.

The apartment was as clean and shiny as Anna herself, with a few spare and tasteful pieces of furniture from Pottery Barn. There was a pretty blue-and-white striped sofa, and the beige carpet was sparkling clean. Unlike my apartment, which was a colorful mélange of things cobbled together from church and yard sales, Anna's exuded a cool, coordinated, and understated air. All of her photos—lots of photos—were neatly organized into pretty floral and striped photo boxes in pastel colors, each box carefully labeled. Her clothes were all from the Gap, mostly denim with tops and sweaters in soothing pastels. She drove a shiny silver Toyota Corolla, a hand-me-down from her father, and often offered me rides here and there.

I was discovering that most American students like Anna started out in college with a lot of things that they'd acquired from their parents, from discarded furniture to old cars. And it was a rite of passage for undergraduate students to routinely go shopping with their parents at Target and Bed, Bath and Beyond to furnish their dorm rooms. Not so for us international students. When we came to the US, our entire life was contained in what two suitcases could hold. There were no parents to turn to. It was just us, figuring it all out, one day at a time.

On leaving India, my suitcases had contained clothes, spices, books, bric-a-brac, and soft 100 percent cotton sheets bought from a shop at the local bazaar in Bhopal. But despite all the efforts to save money and bring all the essentials I could from home, the sheets were always a reminder that I was in a different country. The sheets were made to fit Indian-sized mattresses whose dimensions, it turned out, were different from the American ones. When I got tired of tugging at the corners to make them fit, I bought cheap polyester ones from Kmart because I could not afford the pure cotton ones.

Anna's parents had not only helped her get all set up in Raleigh, but she was still on their health insurance plan and could remain on it right up until the age of twenty-six if she wished. This struck me as a contradiction: On the one hand, developing independence was a prized American value—the earlier the better—and young Americans were considered independent and encouraged to leave home as early as seventeen. And yet for other convenient and practical purposes, they were considered their parents' dependents right into adulthood and remained on their parents' health insurance plans until their late twenties.

ANNA COULDN'T HAVE been more different from Laura and Cathy, two very young women whose apartment was right across from ours. Laura's faded denim shorts barely skimmed her behind, and she favored simple but tight white T-shirts that clung to her perky breasts. Her long blond hair hung down in a mane. Her two-year-old daughter, Missy, had the same hair, but it clung in soft baby curls to her neck. The two women had a boyfriend each, Chuck and Jim, who would together drive up occasionally in a large pickup truck twice the size of Scott's pickup. It was fitted with oversize tires, and Lynyrd Skynyrd blared from the open windows. Chuck often went shirtless, his chest tanned and sinewy above his low-slung faded jeans, a tat-too clearly visible on his left upper arm.

Laura and Cathy would skip out and join them in the pickup truck, cracking open bottles of beer and smoking. While the four of them lounged about in the truck, their laughter ringing through the parking lot, little Missy ran up and down the side-walk, chattering to herself. Chuck was the father, and I often heard raised voices and shouting from inside their apartment when he visited. "Get the fuck out of here," Laura would yell, loud enough for all of us to hear. Missy's wails would eventually drown out the screaming, followed by the roar of Chuck's tires as he drove away.

Unlike the rest of us in Glendale Village, Laura and Cathy were not students, and no one knew what they did for a living. They came and went at odd hours. "I think they're strippers," my neighbor Ashish would say, as Vikram and he sat on the stoop outside our building, eyeing the two women in their skimpy shorts.

Laura and Cathy were different from Anna, different from the Americans in my class. Back in India, everyone thought that all Americans were highly educated and well off—the US was, after all, the land of large, sprawling universities, a beacon of knowledge and learning with the prosperity that education guaranteed. But from what I could tell, neither Laura nor Cathy had even completed high school, and they didn't seem to have much money either. Even though they had a roof over their heads and cars to drive, I guessed that they were perhaps the American version of poor. They were, I would learn, what Amer-icans referred to as "trailer trash."

∽

I PUT ON a gray printed dress that downplayed my ample chest but showed off my relatively slim legs. Anna had invited me to join her for a social group that met on summer evenings. It was a potluck dinner in the home of a Mr. and Mrs. Gordon—John and Stella—who owned a large house in a neighborhood close to the university. There were several cars parked in the driveway and along the road leading to the house. I hung back, a few steps behind Anna, waiting for her to lead the way and introduce me.

The hallway opened into a large dining area where at least twenty-five people were gathered, most of them my age, all of them white.

"Hey everyone, this is my friend, Rajeeka," announced Anna. She continued to mispronounce my name, as did most Americans.

Mrs. Gordon clutched my hand and gushed, "We're so happy you could come."

It was a warm North Carolina summer evening, and everyone gathered in the large garden with the usual red Solo plastic cups in hand, but they contained soft drinks—I noticed that there was no alcohol, which was unusual at such gatherings. Soon the chatter died down, and a hush fell over the group. We all held hands and formed a large circle. Mr. Gordon stepped into the circle.

"Welcome, friends. Stella and I are so happy to welcome you back into this fold and we are honored that the Lord has chosen us for this task."

"Amen, amen," muttered everyone. I glanced sideways. Anna's eyes were closed in rapt attention or perhaps prayer. Mr. Gordon's voice rose louder and louder, followed by an occasional

"Amen." I realized I was listening to a sermon, and while I believed in God and wasn't an atheist by any means, Mr. Gordon's rising voice and the chanting of the group made me nervous. In their fervor, they seemed no different from the religious groups in India that had made me uncomfortable because they proclaimed the superiority of their religion over others. Why had Anna brought me here? I was a Hindu, not a Christian, and it seemed wrong to be a part of this clearly religious gathering, feeling pressured to participate in a ritual that they were all familiar with and to chant "Amen." I rarely even chanted "Om."

To my relief, the sermon finally ended, and we made our way indoors. I hovered in the doorway, feeling even more out of place than I had before. I felt a tap on my shoulder and turned. It was a young Indian man. He must have joined the gathering late, because I could have sworn I was the only nonwhite person there.

"Hey, I'm Steve." I shook his hand. "So how come you're here?" he asked.

"Oh, I'm just here with my friend Anna. She invited me along."

"So, you're not a Baptist?" he asked.

I shook my head. "Nor are you," I said, wondering whether he too had been dragged here by a well-meaning American friend.

"Actually, I am," he said. "I'm a born-again Christian. It's been just amazing to have got my faith back, and this stuff is wonderful."

I didn't know what "born-again" meant, but I realized that "Steve," as he was now known, had given up Hinduism in favor of a newfound faith. He seemed so content with his choice that I didn't have the courage to ask "Why?" Why would an all-Indian fellow (from Vidisha, a small town in the Indian heartland, as I soon learned) convert to Christianity?

Christianity had actually been a powerful presence during my Indian childhood. For a hundred years or more before India's independence from the British, many Hindus and tribal communities in India, particularly those who were poor, had been converted forcibly by the British or coerced by smiling, benevolent missionaries. And even for those of us who were not "converted Christians"—as such communities were known in India—Christianity was everywhere. All my friends and I had at some point in our childhood attended a missionary school. Every small town and big city in India had its own version of St. Joseph's convents, Martyr Day and Holy Child schools, run by gentle nuns and sisters, where grace was dutifully said before every meal even though most of the students didn't understand what they were saying and why they were saying it.

But here was Steve, having chosen to be a Christian. I wondered whether he too had been prodded by his American friends —perhaps subtly—to come to such gatherings, to consider embracing their religion instead of his? Was this a new and modern form of conversion?

I now began to realize the purpose behind the brightly illustrated *Watchtower* magazines that had begun to mysteriously appear in my mailbox, and the groups of people who would go knocking from door to door, the Jehovah's Witnesses. Each time I opened the door to them, they would politely ask: Is the man of the house home? (No, he was not.) I would later learn that, on many US campuses, groups such as the International Church at Yale and International Students in Colorado had for many years idea ?

been reaching out to international students, drawing them into their fold by providing just the type of help that we international students felt we needed to survive during our first several months in a completely foreign place—learning the culture, learning how to shop in American stores, learning how to open a bank account, learning how to drive.

I found myself wondering about the way religion had made its way into the cultural transition I was experiencing. Did Christianity provide an anchor, a sense of belonging, for foreign students who otherwise felt lonely and isolated in enclaves like Glendale Village? Perhaps Steve was simply exercising his right to choose in a country that seemed to be all about having choices: choosing what to study, how to live, and even choosing to shed the shackles of a religion that one was born into.

6

Learning to Drive

"You have to press down the clutch and release the accelerator at the same time," Vikram said, in an exasperated tone.

"You think I don't know that?" I shouted back at him, my face flushed from my repeated attempts to put our car in motion.

When the time had come for us to buy a car, Vikram had declared that we would of course buy a stick shift. That's how the real world drove; automatics were for wimps. Now here I was, for the first time in my life, learning not only to steer a car, but also to operate three pedals simultaneously. I tried one more time, releasing the clutch too quickly, the car jolting to a stop for the fifth time that morning. I pressed my eyes into my hands and started to cry.

"I can't do this, I just can't do this," I said.

Learning to drive felt like one of the hardest things that I had ever had to do. I had never sat behind a steering wheel. Clutch, accelerator, none of it meant anything to me. First the computer, then the car. It was all too much, and all too new.

But I had no choice about learning how to drive. I had learned very quickly upon arriving in the US that owning a car was not a luxury but a necessity. In India, a car was a symbol of upward mobility; a *gaadi*—ideally a chauffeur-driven one—and a large *bangla* to live in were signs that one had arrived. But here in Raleigh it was almost impossible to live without a car. The campus bus ran on limited routes, the public buses were infrequent, and there were no trains. No one seemed to walk anywhere other than on campus itself. It was getting difficult to ask Nehir repeatedly for rides, even though she was willing to take me along for grocery shopping and errands. Her driving was erratic, and I didn't feel safe in her car. So Vikram and I saved every dollar we could with two clear goals: to buy a car and to buy two return tickets to India so that we could visit our families next summer.

Now spending on a cup of coffee felt frivolous, but buying a car wasn't.

GROWING UP, I was always embarrassed that my parents didn't have the sorts of mansions and chauffeur-driven cars that most kids at Sanawar seemed to have. Their parents would drive up to school in long, sleek cars, while my mother and father would cobble together train rides, bus rides, and car shares to be able to come up to my school to meet me. By then my parents were divorced, and I would sometimes fantasize that my mother would remarry, and that my future stepfather would have a fancy home with a fleet of cars and drivers. I would go home on school breaks to a house in one of the posh enclaves of South Delhi, its windows fitted with air conditioners, the air cold enough to give one goose bumps. The chilled crisp air and the car with a chauffeur represented the ultimate in luxury to me.

But that never happened. My mother bought her first car on her own and not until 1991, when she was forty-three, just a year before I came to the US. Until then, we walked a lot. Our weekly excursions to the vegetable bazaar in T.T. Nagar market were on foot. Taking an auto-rickshaw both ways cost too much, so my mother reserved that comfort for the way back, when our baskets were full. Although I later realized that the distance was not as great as I had imagined, back then it felt like an ordeal as we crossed roads with heavy traffic, walking past the British Council library, the small Hanuman temple set into a large banyan tree, and the rows and rows of *jhuggies* or shacks that flanked the steep road leading to the market. Once the shopping was done, after much bargaining over every kilo of vegetables, it was time to argue and haggle with the auto-rickshaw driver whose meter was invariably conveniently broken and who demanded whatever fare he pleased, especially when he saw a woman by herself with a child and without the protective presence of a man.

My father had a car, a light green Fiat, for most of his adult life, but he used it sparingly, always watching the costs of fuel and wear and tear on the precious car that no one other than he could touch. When we lived in Bhopal while I was still a child, riding in my father's car was a rare treat. Mostly, we went about on his Bajaj Vespa-style scooter, with my mother seated at the back in her billowing sari and me sandwiched between the two. Moreover, my father always believed in walking as a form of exercise. He eventually sold his car and walked everywhere, even between his flat and his office in the sweltering heat of Bombay. His shirt would be wet with perspiration by the time he arrived at work. The more he insisted we walk everywhere, the more I longed for the luxury of a car.

VIKRAM, ON THE other hand, had grown up with cars and was used to being in them. He'd arrived at our first date in Delhi in a chocolate-brown Maruti, the kind of small compact car that was quickly replacing the stately, lumbering Ambassador that was a left over from India's colonial past. My friends crowded around the college gate, nudging each other and giggling, as Vikram opened the passenger door for me and I slid into the seat. The air in the car was cool and smelled of his crisp cologne. He handed me a bunch of fresh tuberoses. I was impressed. I later learned that he'd had to beg his older brother to lend him the car for that afternoon, and for many more to come.

Soon Vikram got to be known amongst the hostel girls as the "boyfriend with the car." The brown Maruti became our ally, omnipresent on all our dates, silent witness to our first kiss, and the cool chariot that would whisk me away from the hustle and bustle of Delhi and—at least for the brief duration of a ride—allow me to dream about a future of cool interiors and air conditioners.

Vikram felt happy when he could drive me around in comfort in that little brown car and would cringe each time he had to drop me at the bus stop for the long ride home in a crowded bus to my grandparents' place or back to my college. In his social circle, no one traveled by public transportation. Worst of all was traveling in the economy coach of a train, which we status-conscious Indians referred to as the second-class compartment, a carryover from the strict hierarchy of the British. Or the "cattle class" compartment, as one family friend called it, raising her shapely eyebrows above the rim of her glasses in surprise upon learning that there were still people who couldn't afford to travel any better.

A large part of me felt ashamed and awkward about the class differences between Vikram and me. But part of me wanted to remind Vikram that I wasn't as well off as his family and, whether or not he liked it, this was who I was and he needed to be comfortable with it. But I didn't have the words or the maturity to say it quite that way. So I said nothing and continued to take the awful Delhi Transport Corporation buses and travel second class, despite his sense of discomfort about it.

It now fell to Vikram to teach me how to drive the small white car that we had purchased in Raleigh for what felt like a substantial amount: $800. It was a used Subaru Justy, tiny and compact—just like the brown Maruti—but with room for at least two large suitcases in the back. This was important, for we anticipated many trips to the airport. The Justy was perfect for us.

COOKING WAS ANOTHER survival skill that I needed to master. I had arrived in the US knowing only how to boil an egg and make Indian-style brewed tea. I had never had the need or the occasion to cook. Contrary to the ads I saw on American television of mothers and children baking cookies together, an Indian kitchen was the uncontested domain of adult women. Middle-class Indian children of my generation grew up with grandmothers, mothers, and maids who cooked, and whatever we absorbed of our cuisine was subliminal and based on accidental observation rather than actual, hands-on experience.

Vikram had been in Raleigh for a year before me and was by now proficient in a limited repertoire of staple Indian dishes:

daal, kidney beans, rice, and one of his family's signature dishes, spiced, dry-roasted potatoes. We subsisted on these dishes and my creative experimentation, which included odd combinations such as baked beans and sliced hot dogs, and sandwiches, lots of sandwiches. I soon discovered bologna, the staple of cheap American lunches, made even more nutritionally questionable by the white bread we bought in large loaves from Food Lion. Vikram, meanwhile, discovered Little Debbie Swiss Rolls, devouring the sinful chocolate and cream rolls two at a time. I was too new to the US then to know about the food debates that were already raging about the proliferation of junk food and the ethics and economics of healthy eating.

Our neighborhood Food Lion was about a mile down the road, a sprawling supermarket that took up almost the entire block of the Avent Ferry Shopping Center, along with a laundromat and a Supercuts hair salon. Our weekend routine involved dropping the laundry into a couple of machines at the laundromat and then shopping for groceries at Food Lion.

I awaited these weekend excursions eagerly. I would walk through each aisle marveling at the mind-boggling array of different types of conveniently packaged foods where there was ten of everything. When my wealthy aunt traveled from India to the US on holiday, she would come back raving about the vegetables that were all prepared and ready to use. I had never quite believed her until now. Canned vegetables, chopped vegetables, frozen vegetables, and of course the fresh ones, whose size and perfection seemed unnatural. The bell peppers came not only in four different colors, but were huge and unblemished, nestled in a glistening stack. Yogurt came in the plain form, but I was taken with the little cups with fruit at the bottom. Here, before me again, was that treasured American value of choice, embodied this time in the aisles of a supermarket.

But while I loved perusing each item, my head swimming with all the possibilities, I usually bought just the staples: white bread, butter, jam, yogurt, and cans of frozen OJ which we converted into vats of juice, each of which would last us a whole week. To these supplies we would add the legumes and beans we had brought from India, along with fresh ground spices in sealed bags. It was only later that we discovered the nearby Bhawan Indian Store and realized that it stocked every Indian item imaginable, from Haldiram snacks to Parachute Coconut Hair Oil and even Parle tea biscuits. They were marked up to at least three times their original price in India.

I now knew that one didn't use ketchup on pizza, but there were many other culinary lessons to be learned. One day, while walking from my university department to the library, I was consumed by hunger and allowed myself the rare luxury of stopping in at the convenience store on campus to buy a hot dog. The young woman at the counter handed the hot dog to me and pointed to the different toppings. The ketchup and mustard looked familiar, but there was something that looked like a tangy green minced salad. I spooned a heaping of it on to my paper plate, on the side of the hot dog. I walked up to the counter to pay. The young woman looked at my plate, shook her head, and rolled her eyes.

"Are you sure you want all that relish, honey?"

I nodded, not knowing what else to do. I had already put it on my plate and the line behind me was growing. After that day, I added relish to the list of items that were American condiments, like how Indians ate a bit of pickle on the side with most meals.

Spending a dollar on a cup of coffee seemed like an indulgence when I was saving every penny for my first visit home. But I eventually bought a coffee from the hip café that had just opened on Hillsborough Street, whose paper cups were seen toted all over campus. I scanned the chalkboard menu and finally decided to go all out and order an espresso. I was disappointed when I was handed a tiny paper cup containing an even smaller amount of coffee, as black as anything. There had surely been a mistake, but after the relish episode I felt too self-conscious to say anything. I had expected a delicious coffee with a layer of frothy milk, just like the coffee I used to enjoy at Indian wedding banquets. It took several missteps and some more money spent at cafés to discover that I—or rather we Indians—had our Italian coffee drinks mixed up all along, and that what passed for espresso in India was actually a cappuccino.

While Vikram and I were struggling to learn how to cook and feed ourselves, I noticed that most of the other male Indian students had come up with a clever strategy: they relied on visits from their mothers to provide a supply of fresh, familiar home cooking. Those meals didn't last for just the duration of their mothers' visits. A week or so before the mothers were to go back to India, they would start cooking as if for an army, standing for hours each day in unventilated kitchens, stirring large vats of *daal* and curries and rolling out dozens of rotis. These were then meticulously frozen into portions for later reheating in a microwave, ensuring that their sons wouldn't have to depend on American fast food, God forbid.

The other obvious option was to teach the young men how to cook, just as I was teaching myself, but this was not an idea that seemed to occur to anyone. I wondered if the Indian mums realized that they were raising yet another generation of Indian men who were completely incapable of feeding themselves, or anyone else, for that matter. Daughters, of course, didn't receive such treatment. They were expected to be able to cook and to take care of themselves—and their future husbands.

I MISSED MY mother a lot. I usually called her at night, when it was morning at her end. Most of my mother's sentences began with "here," which was India, or "there," which was America. Those words represented two worlds that couldn't have been more different. My mother would say that she had just finished her daily prayers and was standing by the kitchen window. I could see the kitchen clearly: the gas stove, the array of stainless-steel pots and pans, and the large red LPG gas cylinder.

"Mummy, I can't hear you clearly. What is that sound in the background?"

"*Arre*, have you already forgotten the *subziwallah*?" she would ask.

How could I forget the plaintive call of the vegetable hawker who plies his cart, come rain or shine? As I spoke to her and heard the sounds of everyday life—the hawker, the whistle of the pressure cooker, the barking of our dog—I asked myself what I was doing in the US, so far away from everything I knew. It felt like a schizophrenic existence, my body in one place and my heart in another. We were all living fragmented lives, connected to our homes and families by the telephone and email. I wished I couldn't hear those familiar sounds—that my mother's voice would come from a vacuum, an alien space I had never inhabited and could therefore never imagine, just as she couldn't relate to my surroundings. Although I could see her with painful clarity as she stood in the kitchen complaining about the weather, to her I was a disembodied voice. She didn't know what my apartment in America looked like with its simple desk and lamp, or that my bed was covered with the block-printed cover I'd carried from home.

I LEARNED HOW to cook, and I eventually learned how to drive, mastering the delicate dance between the clutch and the accelerator. On the day of my driving test, I felt nervous as the examiner got into the car beside me. She asked me to drive down a street and down a narrow lane. I looked at Vikram in the rearview mirror for help, but this time I was truly on my own. She then asked me to do a "three-point turn" to get the car out of the impossibly narrow road. It helped that our car was tiny. I turned the steering wheel right, then left, then right, then left, all the while controlling the clutch and accelerator. We finally faced the other way, ready to drive out of the lane, the path ahead of me clear. I had learned how to drive.

In later years, no matter how challenging a drive might be, the one thing I could always pull off was a three-point turn that could get a car out of a tight corner. As for Vikram, after all the fights we'd had during my lessons, he swore that he would never again teach anyone to drive.

7

~~~

A Change of Seasons

A few weeks before, I'd watched with awe as the green leaves outside my bedroom window turned to every shade of orange and red imaginable. Now I watched with a growing sense of sadness as those same leaves fell to the ground, leaving the trees bare and bringing the first chill of the changing season. And just like that, fall passed and it was winter. I pulled out my heavy woolens, gifts from well-meaning relatives in India who imagined that I would need all the warmth possible when moving to the West. But neither they nor I had accounted for indoor heating and that buildings that had been cool during the summer would turn hot and stuffy in the winter, with no need for any covering indoors other than a cardigan. I learned to dress in layers, wearing one piece of clothing over the other so that each could be peeled off with ease. Like an onion.

But our apartment was a different story. As the days got shorter, our apartment got steadily colder. We couldn't afford to pay the high utility bills for increased heating.

"What are we going to do?" I asked Vikram.

"What everyone does," he said, by which he meant all the other international students in Glendale Village. We went to Home Depot and bought large sheets of plastic that we pinned up on each window in our apartment to increase the insulation. I felt sealed in by the plastic, unable to see the sky or the trees outside. I also reverted to the strategies of my schoolgirl days. In Sanawar, up in the Indian mountains, our stone dormitories had no heating. An occasional fire in the fireplace would provide some warmth, but for the most part we were left to our own devices. Before going to sleep, I would don a flannel night suit with long wool stockings underneath, over which I wore another pair of thick socks. I'd then pull a heavy sweater over the entire ensemble and put on a ski cap that covered my entire head other than my eyes, nose, and mouth. Once all the gear was on, I snuggled under the covers, which included a heavy and overstuffed cotton *razai*, and two threadbare blankets on top. This was how the night went, all of us deep within our covers, too cold to talk or to even go to the bathroom. Now the woolen gifts from my Indian relatives came in handy for dealing with my first winter in America.

THANKSGIVING ARRIVED. I was still learning about this uniquely American festival, which invoked gobbling turkeys and expressing gratitude instead of the feverish shopping and gift giving, heralded by numerous newspaper inserts and blockbuster sales, that accompanied most other celebrations in America. I was surprised when Sarah asked me whether we celebrate Thanksgiving in India. I had never heard of the festival before coming to the US and probably for good reason—it was a festival and tradition grounded in America's history.

We were invited to Mary and James Smith's home for a traditional Thanksgiving feast. I'd gotten to know Mary Smith through Vikram. She'd responded to one of the flyers he had put up around the NC State campus, offering his services as a mathematics and statistics tutor. Mary was probably in her mid-forties, returning to school after several years and, like many others in the social sciences, was stumped by the advanced statistical concepts required for her degree.

I was still getting used to the idea of the older graduate student, someone who had accomplished a lot but then decided that they wanted to return to school for further study or to take on a new subject. Farhad Ali and Anne Kessler in my department were two such students. This sort of late-life education was unheard of in India, where most students went through their higher education in one shot: a clear linear sequence of twelve years of schooling, then postgraduate education. There was no question of ever "going back" to school, or even experimenting with different disciplines. It seemed to me a bit self-indulgent that Mary, Farhad, and Anne—grown-ups with so many life responsibilities—were returning to school to pursue additional degrees just because they wanted to.

Mary and Vikram had their first tutoring session on campus. Then Vikram invited her home for the second one, which was to take place on a Wednesday afternoon at 4:00 p.m. I dashed around the apartment, tidying it up. Other than Scott and Amy, we were having an American over to our modest apartment for the first time. Up until now, all our other visitors had been our Indian friends. I peeped through the window and saw Mary's red convertible pull into the parking lot. The first things I noticed were her southern drawl and her kind green eyes. She was dressed trendily in drapes of red and black and I later discovered that she often shopped at Chico's, the go-to store for stylish women of a certain age. Her blond hair was teased and sprayed into a smart bob, and she wore chunky, artistic jewelry.

I offered Mary some tea which she politely declined, pointing to the insulated travel mug in her left hand. I disappeared into the bedroom so that Vikram and she could begin their tutoring session at the wicker dining table. I heard their low voices, mainly Vikram's, as he explained various statistical concepts to her. And then there was a loud shriek. By the time I ran out into the living room, both Vikram and Mary had stepped away from the table and Mary was fanning her face to calm herself.

Unbeknownst to them, a small cockroach—the kind found in the humid American South—had inched its way up the back of the statistics book that Vikram was holding and then sat there, wiggling its antennae at its horrified audience. Vikram and I were terribly embarrassed and apologized to Mary. I didn't know what Mary was thinking, but if I had to guess it would be this: we smelled of spices and our home was dirty, crawling with insects. Every American's stereotype about Indians. Consider the situation: we're living in the American South, which equates Indians with Apu from *The Simpsons*, and the first time an American visitor comes over, we have insects make an appearance. Vikram was quite certain that Mary would never return.

But he was wrong. Not only did Mary return, but their tutoring sessions took on a rhythm—she seemed quite comfortable with being tutored by a young Indian man with a foreign accent and a spartan student apartment. On campus, too, Mary easily befriended other students, always curious about their different backgrounds. Though cosmopolitan in attitude and modern in appearance, Mary was thoroughly Southern in other ways, from her drawl to her charming manners and her strong Christian values. She was, after all, the daughter of a minister and had been born into a family of missionaries.

FOR OUR FIRST Thanksgiving with the Smith family, Vikram and I deliberated over what to wear. My wardrobe was very limited, especially when it came to formal clothing. I had not yet saved up enough to buy any new clothes in America and planned on my default outfit for such occasions: an olive-green skirt with a bias cut, a full-sleeved blouse, and a fitted vest with a flowery print that tied at the back. Vikram wore slacks with a navy-blue blazer and tie. All his bespoke suits and blazers had been tailored by Moolchand Tailors in Delhi, India's equivalent of a Savile Row clothier in London.

We got into our white Justy and drove toward Wilson, where the Smiths lived. Wilson was the heart of the tobacco country in North Carolina and in the nineteenth century had been widely known as the "World's Greatest Tobacco Market." But the Smiths weren't in the tobacco business. James had inherited a real estate company that he now ran.

We pulled up outside a large colonial-style house. It was a gray, overcast day and I shivered in my short wool coat as I stepped out of the car. I hadn't known what to bring since Thanksgiving wasn't a holiday where one exchanged gifts. So I had picked up a small gift hamper from Kmart that contained some preserves, crackers, and other overpriced edibles.

Mary and James both came to the door.

"May I take your pocketbook?" asked James. I looked at him blankly. Vikram nudged me and whispered, "He means your purse." This was another Americanism that puzzled me. There is nothing remotely pocket-like or compact about the large handbags we women typically carry.

The Smiths' house was opulent. It was the first time that I was seeing such a grand American home from the inside, one that resembled the interiors from the TV soap opera *The Bold and the Beautiful*, minus the coastal views. The walls were painted in deep, rich colors, and large, upholstered wingback armchairs sat in the corners of the rooms, flanked by table lamps of gilt and black.

The Smiths' two children, Dallas and Brady, came over to greet us, and I couldn't help thinking that their uncommon names also sounded straight out of an American soap opera. Dallas chewed gum and looked bored; Brady indulged us with small talk.

For all her graciousness as a host, Mary hated to cook, so we headed off to the Wilson Country Club for a traditional Thanksgiving meal. The Smiths drove in their large Buick and we followed in our car. Vikram and I were the only two people of color in the rarefied surroundings of the country club. I felt completely out of place and imagined that all eyes were on us. To top it all, Vikram was a vegetarian—in a Southern town, at a Thanksgiving feast, where massive stuffed, roasted turkeys were the centerpiece on each table.

But the place and its snooty atmosphere reminded me of another such club, thousands of miles away: the Delhi Gymkhana Club, India's most exclusive private club, a British-era leftover with an imperial air and a current waitlist of thirty-seven years to get in as a member. This is where on summer days ladies in impeccable chiffon saris, pearls, and oversize designer sunglasses lounged on manicured lawns, sipping shandies. To simply be able to say that one belonged to the gymkhana, or knew someone who belonged, was to signal that one had arrived. Back in India, our families were members of these types of clubs, but here, in Wilson, Vikram and I felt like interlopers.

After that Thanksgiving, Mary and James became our American family. They were there at my master's graduation when my parents couldn't be there, beaming proudly and gifting me a silver tennis bracelet with a charm in the shape of a scrolled diploma. I was able to enjoy my first holiday on the North Carolina coast when they handed me the keys to their vacation home in Wilmington, and I had my first glimpse of the mountains when I visited their cottage in Blowing Rock, a quaint town nestled in the Blue Ridge Mountains. Through them I saw for the first time how upper-class Americans lived.

Every once in a while, though, I wondered if Mary and James valued us for who we were—two young Indian students, almost two decades younger than them, with viewpoints and experiences very different from theirs—or was their largesse in some ways patronizing? Did they see us as two poor and struggling students from a third-world country who needed to be taken under their wing? I wondered, too, about all the American host families who opened their homes to international students, especially on American holidays like Thanksgiving. Was it a generous effort to expand their own worldview and share their culture, or was it an attempt to indoctrinate what they viewed as lesser cultures into the American way of life? I suppose it was a bit of both.

FALL TURNED INTO the Christmas season. Thanksgiving had brought out decorations in an array of oranges and browns emblazoned with grinning pumpkins and even Halloween-themed buttons and earrings. Now, we were assaulted with red and green everywhere, the smell of potpourri and fruity candles in the air. The office secretaries on campus sported bright, emerald-green business suits, matching heels, and candy cane earrings. This notion of a specific color palette for a specific season was alien to me. The combination of green and red had no special significance in India, where Christmas was more about lights and decorations rather than color-coded apparel. I now understood why when I had worn a favorite green-and-red checked plaid dress in October, people had given me odd glances. I had tucked that dress into the back of my cupboard, but now pulled it out as my new Christmas outfit.

We had no special plans for Christmas and no money to spend on the holiday. But one evening, a few days before Christmas, there was a knock on our door. It was Scott and Amy, surprising us with a large Christmas tree which they had hauled over in Scott's truck along with a string of lights and some ornaments. We set up the tree in a corner of the living room where it almost touched the low ceiling. The fresh smell of pine filled the apartment, and I was grateful to have a real tree that we couldn't have otherwise afforded. We posed before it and took some photos to send home.

I missed India and felt homesick. Even though we were Hindus, I had always been surrounded by the traditions and rituals of Christmas as far back as I could remember. I thought of my mother, curled up in bed on Christmas Eve as she tuned her radio to the BBC to hear carols and hymns. I knew all the Christmas carols by heart because of Sanawar, where a group of us went caroling from dormitory to dormitory just before the school closed for the Christmas vacation. I hadn't read the Bible, nor did I know about the Holy Trinity or the story of the birth of Jesus, but I knew all the words to "We Three Kings" and "God Rest Ye Merry, Gentlemen."

Some Indians believed that Christianity had arrived when Thomas the apostle visited the southern Indian state of Kerala in 52 CE. Sixteen centuries later, Roman Catholicism was brought to India by European colonialists. By the time I was a child, Christianity had become the third-largest religion in India. Christians made up 2.3 percent of the population in India, which doesn't sound like a lot until you realize that in a large country like India that means more than thirty million people.

We had Christians in our family, too. Much to the dismay and horror of my grandparents, my maternal uncle had married Veronica, or Vicky, a Christian lady from the city of Jabalpur. But the story of Christianity in Vicky Aunty's family was different from that of either the Keralites or Catholics. Theirs was a newer history of conversion, in which scores of Indians agreed to become Christians in exchange for jobs and acceptance by the ruling British establishment.

Each Christmas, my mother and I would visit Alok Uncle and Vicky Aunty in Jabalpur. Preparations for the holiday would be in full swing: all the women were baking rose cookies, rainbow cakes, and plum cakes, while Vicky Aunty's brother, Tony, was making hand-stuffed sausages for the occasion. Each evening we would gather at Vicky Aunty's mother's home, put

on the Bee Gees and Boney M., and dance the Hustle and the
Bus Stop, the taller cousins lining up behind the younger ones. It
was the seventies, and no one questioned the pluralism of Indian
culture. All the country's religions coexisted peacefully, each
with its own unique rituals and traditions, with the Hindus as
the unquestioned majority.

But by December 1992, the situation had changed. Tensions
between Hindus and Muslims had been growing for several
years, and on December 6, a mob of angry right-wing Hindus
demolished a Muslim holy site known as the Babri Masjid, a
sixteenth-century mosque which they believed was constructed
over a holy Hindu site. From thousands of miles away in Raleigh,
I followed the news of orange-clad men armed with sticks and
every weapon imaginable, smashing the dome of the historic
mosque, trying to erase India's multireligious history while also
charting a new and militant form of Hinduism—*Hindutva*, or
the supremacy of Hindus. The incident sparked riots between
Hindus and Muslims throughout India, and by the time the unrest subsided, two thousand people had died. Watching the
news, I felt a deep chill that had nothing to do with the bitter
December cold in North Carolina.

As the rift between Hindus and Muslims grew back in India, so did a sense of division between Vikram and me. I was
slowly beginning to realize that, even though we were both
from the same religion, our views were very different. I found I
was beginning to ask myself some probing questions about my
attitudes toward religion. What was the meaning of religious
freedom? Did I believe in the supremacy of one religion over
others? Was it necessary to follow religious rituals? Where
would I draw the line between charming traditions and op-

pressive practices that—although cloaked in holiness—were often ways of subjugating women?

None of these were questions I had thought to ask earlier. Nor had I raised any of these issues with Vikram before I'd entrusted my heart to him. At the age of nineteen, I had simply seen his cute smile, inhaled his aftershave, enjoyed the drives in his air-conditioned car, and swooned over his deep voice and dexterity with the guitar. I didn't ask about his thoughts on women and work (even though he came from a family of highly accomplished and well-educated women), and I never probed his religious views.

Now we began to talk about these topics, and I found myself becoming uncomfortable with some of Vikram's responses. We seemed to be evolving in two different directions—growing in our individual ways, but growing apart as a couple.

8

Patel-Motel: Indians in America

I t was time for me and my classmates to choose the research topics for our master's theses. By now I had discovered that I could
take courses outside of traditional psychology, the program in
which I was enrolled. The ability to study different subjects that
went beyond my chosen major seemed to be a unique feature of
American-style education, and I took advantage of this flexibility
to learn more about economics and global development. Coming
from India, where almost two-thirds of the population lives on
less than three dollars a day, the overabundance of the US—where
college students who were ostensibly struggling shopped at Gap
and drove their own cars—baffled me. I was becoming acutely
aware of this stark contrast in affluence and "economic development," and education seemed to play a big role in it.

Under Dr. Bishop's guidance, I had become interested in how
women's education was linked to all sorts of positive outcomes,
from the educational level of their children and their family's
health to their ability to be economically independent. In the US,
most girls and women were educated, but in India only seven out
of ten girls and women received any sort of schooling, among the
lowest rates in the world, which meant that female literacy was a
pressing issue and serious social problem. These facts mirrored

what I had observed in India: most of the women who were domestic workers, or sold fruits and vegetables at the market, or worked as migrant laborers in cities were unable even to sign their names, using an inked thumbprint instead.

Motivated by these reflections, I decided to write a master's thesis about rural women in India and the type of education available to them. I wanted to find out what happened when village women were formally educated.

"I'm going to focus on women and education in India," I announced to Anne Kessler.

"But I thought you were interested in Asia," she said, looking surprised.

"But India is in Asia," I said. This was not the first time that I'd heard an American questioning the "Asian-ness" of India. Each time I eagerly turned to a newspaper report about Asian Americans with the hope of learning something more about Indians in America, I found that the definition of "Asian" was limited to those with roots in East Asia, or at most in Southeast Asia. "Asian food" was, by default, Chinese, or Japanese, Korean, or Vietnamese, which seemed to be as far as the American geographic imagination dared to stray. What geographic space did the entire region of South Asia or the Indian subcontinent— including India, Nepal, Bangladesh, Pakistan, Bhutan, and Sri Lanka—occupy in the minds of most Americans? Where would an American schoolchild point to a map when trying to pick out these places? I wondered.

The US Census Bureau's definition was more accurate. It defines an Asian as a person having origins in any of the original peoples of the Far East, Southeast Asia, or the Indian subcontinent, including, for example, Cambodia, China, India, Japan, *contemporary v historical* ⊘

Korea, Malaysia, Pakistan, the Philippine Islands, Thailand, and Vietnam. And I discovered that, among these communities, Indians were one of the fastest growing groups of new immigrants to the US, second in number only to the Chinese. The Indian American population has expanded by 110 percent between 2005 and 2015, reaching almost four million.

Perhaps India's omission from America's collective consciousness of Asia was rooted in the complicated racial history and exclusionary laws of the US. Indians looked distinctly different from other Asians and were excluded from the 1882 law that barred Chinese immigrants from entering the US. But Indians were impacted by the Immigration Act of 1917, in which the US Congress created the Asiatic Barred Zone, effectively stopping the flow of five hundred million people from all of Asia— the "yellow peril" and "tide of turbans," along with "idiots," "epileptics," and others that were seen as threatening to taint America.

How Americans viewed the origins of Indians like me was also an unfortunate legacy of historical errors and colonial misdeeds. When Christopher Columbus landed in the exotic and balmy Bahamas in 1492, he thought he had discovered the East or India, which is what he had set out to do, and so he called the island's inhabitants "Indians." After Columbus's first voyage to this region, Europeans adopted the term "West Indies" to distinguish the region from the "East Indies," or India and the East. But referring to Indians as "East Indians" was always a misnomer. There is no actual region or place called "East India," and to call someone an "East Indian" is simply incorrect. There is India and the Indian people—a simple reality that, unfortunately, many Americans seem to find confusing.

Yet despite being a bit misunderstood and occasionally invisible, Indians in America—as international students or otherwise—seemed to be doing something right. We had managed to develop a stereotype of being intelligent, hardworking, and successful. In other words, we were the "model minority," along with other Asian Americans.

As I got to know the Indian American community, I realized that there was an element of truth in this stereotype. Everywhere I looked—whether it was professors, scientists, engineers, doctors, investment bankers, researchers—Indians seemed to excel in most things that we took on, and this despite the early challenges in American classrooms and having to adjust to a whole new way of learning and functioning. Indians were the best-educated group in the US, with 72 percent holding a college degree or higher as compared with 51 percent of all Asian Americans and 30 percent of all Americans. Indian Americans also had the single highest income level of any group in the country, more than double that of the general US population. Conversely, Indians were half as likely to be living in poverty as compared with all Americans.

As I pursued my study of global development and pondered the extreme poverty in India, I puzzled over the success and affluence of those Indians that had left India and come to the US. What was the secret to our success? Was it something to do with Indians, or was it something about the US that enabled us to succeed despite considerable odds?

Gradually, I concluded that it was a bit of both. There was of course the famous Asian work ethic and perseverance. Indian families, much like most other Asians, placed a premium on hard work. Indian students like me embodied our families' aspirations, always aware of the personal and financial sacrifices that had transported us this far.

But the reasons for our success in America went beyond this cultural exceptionalism. Like thousands of Indian students before me, I had benefited from a unique confluence of privileges that Kapur and his colleagues have referred to as "triple selection." First, we'd had the opportunity to attend India's top-tier educational institutions, where we received solid undergraduate schooling imparted in English from professors who had often been trained abroad.

Second, many of us also came from families that already enjoyed a high social status. India had a strict social hierarchy, and where one appeared in the rank order was based on an implicit formula that included whether or not someone spoke with the right English accent; where one had been to school; and whether or not one dressed in the right clothes. Unlike the US, where the external markers of social and economic difference were less visible—it was hard to tell whether a black T-shirt was from Old Navy or from Abercrombie and Fitch—in India these differences were visible and evident, a resume of one's heritage and social capital (or lack thereof) that each of us carried around.

I was very aware of this privilege, which I derived not so much from my family's modest wealth but from my education—the fact that I had attended one of India's most elite boarding schools, spoke impeccable English, and had a mother who was an English professor and a father who was a top journalist for India's major English newspapers. Even without being rich, my family's academic and professional background and dropping the name of my school opened many doors.

The final form of advantage from which many Indian

Americans benefited was the way in which the Indian Institutes of Technology (IITs)—India's twenty-three elite and rigorous engineering institutions—served as launching pads for students eager to pursue further education at top US colleges and universities and then the American dream. Between 1953 and 2006 alone, nearly twenty-five thousand IIT graduates settled in the US, and it is estimated that one in four IIT graduates ends up going to the US. My neighbors Ashish and Ravi were both products of the IIT pipeline. And for every Indian engineering student in NC State's science and engineering departments, there was at least one Chinese student. The joke went that at lunchtime most computer labs at NC State smelled of either Chinese food or Indian curry.

Unfortunately for me, the IIT privilege didn't extend to psychology majors. The easy comfort that the Indian students felt in the engineering departments was quite different from my experience, where I was the token Indian in my department, at once exotic and peculiar.

IT WAS NO accident but rather a carefully crafted US national policy of selection and exclusivity that allowed educated, talented Indians to succeed in the US. The gathering momentum of the civil rights movement in the US led to the Immigration and Nationality Act of 1965, which ended racist immigration laws that discriminated based on national origin. We Indians directly benefited. Where once South Asians were the "least desirable race of immigrants thus far admitted to the United States" who could not own or lease land or become naturalized US citizens, the 1965 act ushered in a new generation of the "best and brightest" from around the world, including many highly educated professionals and students from India.

It was this second wave of Indian immigration that brought Uncle Satish to the US, along with successive generations of Indians and other international students from all over the world. Yet a strange thing happened: while the 1965 act was highly selective and based on attracting the very best, it had the unintended consequence of leveling the playing field amongst us Indians once we had arrived in the US. While back home the social boundaries separating different Indians were clearly drawn, they were blurred in the US—to most Americans we Indians were all one and the same, foreigners and outsiders who looked and sounded different. Our shared foreignness unified all the Indian students across campus in the most unexpected of ways. No one was judged any longer by their last name (which in turn would reflect their caste and social status), nor by the shade of their brownness, nor by whether or not they spoke English with the proper accent. We were all starting from scratch, building our own versions of the American dream and, as far as America was concerned, what mattered was our talent and our willingness to work hard.

But as I thought about my place in America, of where I sat on the spectrum of Indians, it occurred to me that we were so busy in our steady march toward the good life and so proud of being the model minority that we had forgotten the struggles that had brought us this far, as well as our relationship with other communities in the US. I thought often about the episode in Sarah's class and the Black man I'd unwittingly offended. I wondered why Indians in the US had chosen to distance themselves from African Americans when, in fact, the privileges that we now enjoyed and took for granted were earned on the backs of the civil rights movement. The struggle to end all forms of discrimination had forced the passage of the Immigration Act of 1965 that once again opened the doors to international students and immigrants from India, whom leaders like Martin Luther King saw as compatriots in the struggle for minority rights. Why did we Indians then see ourselves as superior to Black people when in fact we should be in solidarity with them?

THAT DECEMBER, A group of us Indian students decided to drive to Charlotte to visit a friend over New Year's Eve. It was a two-hour drive from Raleigh. The weather forecast called for snow, but we didn't pay much attention to it; after all, it had never snowed in North Carolina the past five years. So off we went on I-40 on a frigid day, classic rock on the dial and bundled into Ashish's old but respectable Honda Accord (nicknamed the Hindu Accord because of its popularity amongst many Indians).

About an hour and a half into our drive, the sky turned a dull steely gray and the first snowflakes began to fall. Then the snow began to come down steadily, blanketing the road and the car. I felt afraid. We had never driven in snow before. I had heard of snow tires and chains, but we didn't have those winter accessories. Ashish slowed the car to a crawl. The visibility dropped and all I could see ahead were the fuzzy taillights of an 18-wheeler tractor trailer. Our car began to weave lightly over the ice and snow covering that was forming on the road. I recalled a question from my written driving test: Which way should you turn your steering if your car is skidding? It had seemed like an academic question then, but here we were now, navigating an increasingly slippery road.

An exit sign said LEXINGTON 1 MILE. "Let's get off here," said Ashish.

Suddenly a car ahead of us, much like ours, veered from its lane and slid under the 18-wheeler in the lane next to it. I pressed my face into my hands just as I heard the crunch of the metal against the tires. *Please, God, just get us safely to Lexington,* I prayed. I had never heard of Lexington before, but at that moment I was convinced that it was our last refuge from the icy highway.

Inch by inch, we got closer to the exit. We made it onto a side road where we saw a gas station and a Comfort Inn. We gently pulled into the parking lot of the motel. The doorbell pealed as we entered, and the man at the front desk looked up. He was Indian. A glimmer of recognition crossed his face, the look that each Indian gives another in a country away from home which says: "I may not know you, but in a larger, universal sense, we know each other, because we come from the same place."

"I don't have any rooms left," he said, before we could even ask. "The weather has just been so bad that many people have pulled off the highway. Let me call some other places for you."

He dialed a few numbers as we waited. Nobody had any rooms. Where would we go? We were in the middle of nowhere, and we were surrounded by big interstate trucks that had pulled off the highway.

"Wait a minute here," the motel clerk said. He went into a private room behind the front desk and re-emerged some minutes later, accompanied by a middle-aged woman.

"I am Mr. Shah and this is my wife. We have discussed this situation and would like you to stay with us as long as you need to. We own this hotel and we have a full apartment in the basement. You're welcome to stay."

The tension drained from my body. I wanted to cry.

"Come, come," said Mrs. Shah, repeating her entreaties as many Indians do.

We followed the two of them to the basement, which had a large ping-pong table and a carrom board. Carrom was a very popular game in India, but I hadn't seen a carrom board in the US. There were two Indian teenagers at the board, and the Shahs introduced them as Nilesh and Neela, their children. They greeted us diffidently and turned back to their game.

Many Indians who had come to the US once the doors to the country reopened in 1965 now had children who had grown up in America. The relationship between Indians like me and these second-generation Indian Americans was proving to be a complex one. Many of them regarded people like me as "fresh off the boat," or FOBs—unsophisticated country bumpkins. On the other hand, we, the "authentic" Indians, tended to regard Indians born in America as ABCDs—American Born Confused Desis—a derogatory term for an American-born person with family roots in India. The mockery didn't end with the first four letters of the alphabet: the Urban Dictionary defined the Indian diaspora as the "American Born Confused Desi Emigrated From Gujarat, Housed In Jersey, Keeping Lotsa Motels, Named Often Patel, Quickly Reaches Success Through Underhanded Vicious Ways; Xenophobic, Yet Zealous." The alphabet captured in just twenty-six words the stereotypes that defined Indian immigrants in the US.

On the NC State campus, the FOBs and the ABCDs did not mix, the latter viewing the former with disdain, averting their eyes each time they encountered Indians from the homeland with their greasy hair, faint curry odor, and unfashionable clothes. Indians like me, with our simple lifestyle and Indian-accented English, must have reminded the young men and women of where their own parents had come from. It would probably take them years of untangling their hyphenated identity as Indian Americans to finally embrace their roots. The process would likely begin with a tentative exploration of their heritage— learning an Indian musical instrument or performing coordinated dance routines to Bollywood music at Indian weddings.

Vikram and Ashish put away their bags and sat down to play carrom with Nilesh and Neela. The battle of the ABCDs vs the FOBs, I thought. In no time, the flat discs were whizzing across the board and it was as if we had been there forever. We may not have been born in the same country, but we were connected by unique traditions.

I had heard the term "Patel-Motel" used pejoratively to refer to this group of Indian immigrants, but only now understood what it meant. Indian immigrants now owned roughly half of the motels in the country, and most were from just one Indian state: Gujarat. Most were following in the footsteps of Kanjibhai Desai, a Gujarati immigrant who'd acquired a motel in California in the 1940s and had unwittingly hit upon a new business idea for enterprising Gujaratis. Soon, Gujarati-owned establishments began to crop up all over the country—many belonging to well-known all-American chains like Best Western—and often in far-flung towns across the US. And now here we were, in the remote town of Lexington in North Carolina, with a population of just eighteen thousand, and I wondered how it felt for the Shahs to be the only Indian immigrants in this isolated community.

The Shahs hosted us for two days, during which Mrs. Shah

cooked elaborate Indian meals and Mr. Shah regaled us with stories of his early days in America. They were eager to talk because they hardly ever saw another Indian in this part of North Carolina. I learned that the Shahs had come to the US from the western Indian state of Gujarat, seeking a better future. Though Mr. Shah was a practicing doctor in India, he found that it wasn't easy to reestablish himself as a medical professional in the US. He did what many Gujaratis before him had done: he set up a motel franchise which, if not as respectable as the medical profession, was definitely a lucrative one.

We helped Nilesh and Neela wash the laundry and haul the heavy vacuum cleaner around the hotel. When it was time to leave, we promised to stay in touch with our newfound Indian family. Mr. and Mrs. Shah stood beneath the large Comfort Inn sign, waving to us as we drove off. As we got back on I-40, I knew that I would never make Patel-Motel jokes again.

History Lessons

Anna shut the trunk of the car and turned to me. "Ready?" she asked.

"Ready," I said, giving her a thumbs-up sign. It was spring break, and Anna had invited me to join her on a trip to Washington, DC. I was excited. This would be my first long road trip in the US. Vikram seemed skeptical of the whole idea of two young women gadding about, but I wanted to go.

We got on the road at 7:00 a.m.; Anna drove and I navigated. We both wore matching denim shorts, but no one would have mistaken us for twins: with my dark hair, dark eyes, and light complexion, I could pass for Middle Eastern, Spanish, Greek, Indian, or Turkish, while Anna was tall, blond, and blue-eyed.

I rested my head against the seat and looked up through the sunroof at treetops silhouetted against the pure blue North Carolina sky. It reminded me of the day I had flown into Raleigh and traveled this same road in Scott's pickup truck, but that early sense of nervousness had now been replaced with a greater sense of comfort.

"You can't hurry love," crooned Phil Collins on the radio, and I began to sing along. "Wait, how do you know this song?" Anna asked.

"Because I was listening to it in school, just the way you probably were," I said. "I'm a huge fan of cheesy eighties music."

"I had no idea," said Anna. "So, you know, like, Madonna and Michael Jackson?"

"Every song, every lyric," I replied.

In Sanawar, the exchange students from Europe and the US had brought with them the latest music from abroad: Tears for Fears, Michael Jackson, Madonna, A-ha, Eurythmics. We had one small battery-operated tape player for the entire dorm and would huddle around it, mouthing the lyrics. Some of the other Indian girls brought the same music back on cassette tapes, carefully recorded off of radio channels in the US or England, where the cheery voice of the disc jockey informed us that Michael Jackson's "Thriller" had just made it to the top of the charts. We replayed the music until the batteries wore out, and the song became a warbly, low-voltage version of the original.

Now, Anna and I both hummed along to the radio as we headed north, driving through North Carolina and Virginia, past large billboards advertising "gentlemen's clubs" and McDonald's amid the wild greenery.

Four and a half hours later, we were in DC. We drove past the National Mall, flanked by the striking white dome of the Capitol on one end and the tall column of the Washington Monument on the other. The imposing buildings and grandeur reminded me of Rajpath, or the King's Way, the heart of the government in New Delhi, with the stone arch of India Gate at one end of the long road and the Rashtrapati Bhavan and circular Parliament on the other. Each year on January 26, India's anniversary of becoming a republic, Rajpath was the venue of one of the grandest military parades in the world with marching and mounted military contingents, an array of military vehicles, military bands, and an air show by fighter jets, in addition to cultural performances by hundreds of schoolchildren. As a child, I had often watched the grand spectacle sitting astride my father's shoulders.

Anna was keen to see the Holocaust Museum, the latest addition to the numerous museums in DC. I wondered why she was eager to see such a depressing place, and why there would even be a whole museum dedicated to the Holocaust. I had been hearing a lot about the Holocaust ever since arriving in the US. It was a subject I'd previously learned about only through a passing reference to Nazism in my history textbooks in India and having read Anne Frank's diary. Indian history textbooks avoid the term "holocaust" when teaching about the Second World War, and when India's right-wing political party came into power, government-prescribed textbooks omitted any mention of the genocide. Now I was beginning to understand what a huge blind spot this had created for Indians like me.

The United States Holocaust Memorial Museum was a subdued stone building, its austerity a stark contrast to the decorative flourishes of the other museum buildings that flanked the National Mall. How would one describe a museum so somber? Wonderful? Moving? These descriptions seemed too bright and cheerful for the dark history that was contained within the museum.

I walked through a glass corridor where the panes were etched with the names of towns that had been completely wiped out because of the Holocaust. Then I reached the room of shoes —four thousand of them taken from the prisoners arriving at the Majdanek concentration camp in Lublin, Poland. There were men's shoes, women's shoes, children's shoes, and even tiny baby shoes—no one had been spared. Their owners had per-ished, but the shoes had survived, a rubbery smell rising from the heap. A period in history which had seemed almost mythi-cal, far removed from my Indian classrooms by both geography and context, now seemed very real.

I COULDN'T FALL asleep that night. Each time I closed my eyes, I saw the heap of shoes in the museum. They reminded me of other shoes that had been left behind in a hurry in 1947 as my father's family was fleeing what became Pakistan on the stroke of midnight on August 15, when two nations were cleaved from one.

Almost five million Hindus and Sikhs were displaced and forced out of the newly formed Pakistan, while 5.5 million Mus-lims fled what became a Hindu-majority India. By the time the most tumultuous and violent phase of the Partition was over, more than fifteen million people had been displaced—the largest forced migration of its kind in modern history—and a couple of million had died in massacres or in their attempts to flee.

Though both the Holocaust and the Partition were vast human tragedies, they were fundamentally different. There was no one perpetrator in the Partition—Hindus, Muslims, Sikhs all turned against each other, their anger stoked by the machina-tions of the British. It was a "mutual genocide." But the sheer scale of the violence, destruction, death, and horror of the Parti-tion evoked that of the Holocaust, with some suggesting that the atrocities of the Partition were far more barbaric and bloodier.

Just as the memory and narrative of the Holocaust is central to the identity of modern Jewish families in the US, the story of the Partition is woven into the fabric of many Punjabi families' lives in postindependence India, especially those settled in Delhi. Following the Partition, a city that was once the seat of power of Muslim and British Empires was remade into a vast refugee colony, providing a haven to almost half a million Hindus who fled Pakistan, including my father's family.

But despite the magnitude and horrors of the Partition, I was discovering that many Americans did not know about it. There also seemed to be a vast gap in research and literature: There was so much written about the Holocaust, but why not about the Partition? In India, too, other than a handful of films and books, the Partition and its aftermath didn't occupy a place in the social awareness of my generation in India. I wondered: Did we Indians want to erase it from our collective memory? We didn't fully understand the histories of where our grandparents had come from or have a sense of how the ravages of this forced migration—where all was lost—had affected generations to come.

The more I thought about the Holocaust, the more I realized how little I knew about the Partition. I slowly began to piece together my family's history by asking my grandmother about it.

ON MARCH 16, 1936, my grandmother, one among five children, turned twenty. In those days, a girl that age was considered old, fast approaching the end of her marriageable prime. But my grandmother wanted none of it. What she wanted was to play tennis, take long coach rides with her father to Lawrence Gardens in Lahore, and attend college. She became the first woman to graduate from her local university in Jammu, then enrolled for a distance communication course in fine arts from a college in London.

Fearful of having an overeducated and unmarried daughter, her father arranged her marriage with my grandfather, Dharam Pal Bhandari. My grandmother eventually came to terms with domesticity and motherhood, and the Bhandaris had a comfortable and unruffled existence till the Partition. Cocooned in their safe neighborhood in Lahore, they dismissed the growing social unrest as petty squabbles in the city's less desirable areas.

Then, one morning, the newspapers informed them that there was now an India and a Pakistan. They were now Hindus living in a Muslim nation. Overnight, just like that, two nations were forged from one. One by one, the other Hindu families in their neighborhood decided to leave this new Pakistan, a notion as foreign to them as the land was familiar. But my grandfather resisted leaving till they were the only Hindu family left in the neighborhood. Finally, upon the insistence of Mr. Aziz, a Muslim friend, my grandparents agreed to leave early in the morning, in the hour when the air is heavy and still. My grandmother quickly tied up as many things as would fit in a few bundles and small trunks.

My grandparents believed they would be back very soon, that this was a temporary displacement. They did not know then—as the heavy doors of the house closed behind them, as the tonga rounded the bend of Gobind Ram Street, the lane named after my great-grandfather—that their life as they knew it was over. Many years later, after India and Pakistan had fought four wars and thousands of lives had been lost, my grandmother

syntax?
"slowly dre

continued to wonder whether their old Lahore house still stood or if it had been torn down, a lifetime of memories and belongings erased in the creation of a new country.

On August 21, 1947, with a few bundles and three children, my grandparents arrived in Delhi by train. They were fortunate to be alive; many other trains had been attacked en route, their passengers killed and burnt, not unlike many Jews who were also transported to their death in trains during the Holocaust.

As my grandmother looked out of the barred window of the ramshackle third-class train compartment, she did not know that it was her first glimpse of the city where she would live and slowly die over the course of fifty years. But as Delhi began to overflow with thousands of refugees, my grandmother realized that she would never see Lahore again. She never got used to being a refugee, for there had been nothing in Lahore that she had sought refuge from. But Lahore was lost to my grandmother forever; there was no going back, no reclaiming of places or moments.

My grandparents were allotted a plot of land in Delhi in a colony called East Patel Nagar; they were one of many refugee families that settled on their street. As my grandparents struggled with their new life in India, my grandmother learned how to recycle. My father, the oldest child, had barely any clothes— everything had been left behind except for what he was wearing the night they left Lahore. My grandmother began to alter my grandfather's discarded trousers for my father, and when he outgrew them, she would alter them again, shortening them for the next boy in line. Nothing was ever wasted or discarded.

Slowly, over the course of five years, their situation improved. My grandfather obtained a position as a barrister in a respectable law office and bought his first car, a large chocolate-brown Ambassador. They set up a living room, not as grand as the one in Lahore with its carved rosewood furniture, but one with modern furniture of the 1960s that was becoming quite fashionable in Delhi, and the grand old radio around which the family would gather every evening to listen to the newscaster from All India Radio read the latest developments in his grave voice. They finally had enough, not half as much as what they had in Lahore, but enough for the Bhandari family which, by now, had expanded to six people.

But even after things improved, my grandmother never stopped collecting things. To this day, every year when my aunts and uncles—now dispersed as immigrants all over the world—leave their comfortable homes in America, New Zealand, and Australia to visit the musty old house in Patel Nagar, they complain about all the things my grandmother has hoarded and can't seem to let go of: the empty bottles, the useless cups, the unfinished paintings, and the outdated magazines. "Unnecessary clutter," they call it.

But after seeing the Holocaust museum and the remnants of a life that refugees and those who are fleeing leave behind, I finally began to understand the value of mere objects, to understand why it was so important for my grandmother to hold on to everything lest it all be lost again. The histories of the Holocaust and the Partition may have been different, but the ravages were similar. Despite everything she had surrounded herself with, despite the comfortable life she eventually came to lead in Delhi, my grandmother could never reclaim what she had lost in her journey as a refugee.

~~~

THE TRIP WITH Anna to DC led me to learn about my fam͟ ͟⹃͟ɪs-
tory of the Partition. I was also discovering that history was interpreted in various ways depending on where one sat. This was
most apparent to me when it came to Iran and Afghanistan in
the US. Americans seemed to feel very differently about Iran
and Iranians than did Indians back home. In the US, Iranians
were discussed either in hushed tones or with palpable anger,
with Iran regarded as a place of darkness, extremism, and ignorance. It was the same with Afghanistan. To look at Iran and
Afghanistan through American-tinted glasses was to see them as
fundamentally evil and benighted.

But this was not the Afghanistan or Iran I knew. In the collective memory of most Indians, Afghanistan is the land of the
Kabuliwala, Rabindranath Tagore's tale about the fruit seller
from Kabul. Growing up, I associated Afghans with strength of
character and valor. And Iran to me was Persia, a land of art and
poetry, where Isfahan was to the Indian subcontinent what Paris
was to the West, and where Farsi was the equivalent of Latin—a
language of culture and refinement, the poetic language of
Hafez in Persia and Mirza Ghalib in India. My maternal grandfather spoke Farsi not because he was Iranian, but because it was
assumed that educated Indian men of his generation would be
schooled in the lingua franca of the East.

My first exposure to modern-day Iranians was through Tau-
fiq and Fereshteh, graduate students from Iran who had arrived
in the Indian city of Bhopal in 1981 to attend college and were
also learning English from my mother, a professor of English at
the local university. It was soon after the Iranian Revolution,

when the country's westernized and privileged elite fled, heading to the West but also to neighboring countries like India, which has shared a long history with Persia. Thousands of aspiring Iranian students migrated to colleges in India's smaller cities. I didn't know then the political developments surrounding the revolution, but what left an impression on my eleven-year-old mind was Fereshteh's rice *polow*, a steaming and fragrant dish studded with raisins.

In the eighties and nineties, large numbers of Palestinian students also studied in India. I knew Mahmud as just the Palestinian guy who rented a room at the back of our neighbor Mishra Aunty's house, sported a keffiyeh tied around his neck rakishly, and rode a motorcycle. Lacking even a textbook knowledge of the Israeli-Palestinian conflict, I had no context for what his people were going through or why so many of them were finding their way to countries like India that were proving to be a refuge for students. Even though India wasn't a first-world country, students like Mahmud were at least able to get a solid education in English.

The deep suspicion with which most Americans regarded Iranians also ran counter to what I was experiencing firsthand after coming to the US. One of the first students I had met in my department was Farhad, one of four thousand Iranian students in the US that year. Farhad was like the many Iranians I had known in India: kind, soft-spoken, and cultured, with a generosity of spirit that seemed fundamentally Iranian. Then there was Sasha, a businessman whose family generously donated to me— a struggling international student—their plush furniture and antiques when they moved away from North Carolina.

But the context and history of the Indian subcontinent was

clearly not the same as the relationship of the US with all these places. I was beginning to realize that my understanding of Iran was a romanticized one, airbrushed with nostalgia but not rooted in political and national realities. Through my American class-mates I learned more about the Iran hostage crisis and began to better understand the deep anger and resentment of Americans toward Iran, a country they viewed as a hotbed of Islamic fun-damentalism. It was hard to believe that in 1979, the largest number of international students in the US were from Iran, numbering about fifty thousand. The Iranian Revolution of 1979 and the seizure of American hostages at the American Em-bassy in Tehran in 1980, however, changed everything. By 1983, the number of Iranian students in the US had dropped to around twenty-seven thousand, and over the next several years the flow of students from Iran to the US dried up.

I had left home to learn more about America, but leaving home was helping me understand my own country's history bet-ter. It was also teaching me about the contexts, histories, and perceptions of students from all over the world, too. Venturing beyond India was challenging my stereotypes about the world. But it wasn't clear to me whether my American classmates were also developing a broader and deeper understanding of the world beyond their own country's borders.

10

Coupon Queen

When I came to America, the metrics of my existence had changed. I found myself spending a lot of time converting one set of numbers into another. To make sense of the weather, I learned to convert from Celsius to Fahrenheit, and I converted the time of day—when it was morning in Raleigh, it was nighttime in India. But it was money that I wrestled with the most, engaging in an intricate form of mental math. A dollar wasn't just a dollar, it was sixty-five rupees, and to me it represented all that sixty-five rupees could buy in India. I balked at spending ten dollars on a sandwich—650 rupees, the monthly salary for a poor person in India. It all seemed so excessive.

How did my family afford to send me to the US to study? I had been to one of the best schools in India, but that didn't mean that we had a lot of money. I managed to attend it because my mother had attended the same school, and I benefited from legacy admissions as well as from a small scholarship that my father—who had the embarrassing habit of asking for money and financial help even where none was clearly needed or was available—had pestered the school to provide.

When I finished school and began college, even though the University of Delhi was among the top institutions in India, my college education was downright cheap by US standards. My annual fees and tuition were 18,000 rupees, or just $400, according to the exchange rate of the early nineties. The hostel costs were an additional $400. Now, at NC State, my tuition and living costs combined were close to $10,000, and that was considered a deal, as I was paying tuition at the in-state or subsidized rate typically reserved for students from North Carolina. Average costs at other US institutions were much higher. Around me I saw students working two jobs, attending classes part-time, or taking on large loans to be able to attend school full-time.

Like most Indians, I was frugal and debt-averse, and lived within my means even though the income from my assistantship was meager. But my American classmates had nicely furnished apartments and did not seem to be cutting any corners even though they were studying and living on borrowed money— most had taken on huge loans. I gradually came to understand that this is typical of American students. With each passing year, student debt in the US has continued to rise, with 70 percent of all undergraduates leaving college in debt. By some estimates, it would take the average American college graduate close to twenty years to pay back their student debt, a burden second only to home mortgages in the US.

Ordinary student debt wasn't an option for me. As an international student, I wasn't eligible for federal loans in the US, and I also didn't have anyone in the US who could be a cosigner for a private loan. But some Indian students had taken loans back home, or, rather, their parents—who were elderly or retired—had taken loans on their behalf or were cosigners on debt with high interest rates of over 10 percent.

Some years later, when my friend Ashish appeared for an

interview for admission into an MBA program at the University of Texas, Austin—a highly regarded program but still ranked well below the other top MBA programs—he was asked the question: Why did you apply to UT, Austin? There were many reasons, but an important one was the massive debt he would have undoubtedly had to shoulder had he attended a far more expensive business school such as Wharton or Kellogg.

I GRADUALLY LEARNED how to manage my money using the tricks that other Americans used. Each Sunday morning, I waited for the thump of the weekend *News and Observer* being delivered outside the front door. Then, armed with scissors and a cup of tea, I would begin to go through the glossy advertising inserts, which were what interested me the most. I was looking for coupons for shampoo, canned tomato sauce, toilet paper, and all manner of household and personal items. I read the fine print of the coupons carefully so that I could maximize my savings. Our home began to fill with the American brands that I saw advertised on TV. One month it was Finesse shampoo, the next month it was Head and Shoulders, depending on which brand appeared in that month's coupons.

Then there were the buy-one-get-one-free deals, another cornerstone of American retail. But the trick was figuring out that one wasn't in fact paying more for the "buy one" item before getting the other free. American retail practices baffled me, particularly the ability to buy something and then return it just because you changed your mind. And then there was the trust factor—so much in America was based on mutual trust. You could fill your car with gas and then pay the attendant afterward. Americans, I was discovering, were very honest and earnest, hewing close to clearly established social rules. I initially viewed this behavior with suspicion, thinking there must be a catch somewhere. I came from a culture where corruption and bending the rules were almost universal—*jugaad* as it was called, which basically means finding a hack or wielding power, influence, and money to get the job done. By contrast, the simple honesty of Americans was disarming.

That first year at NCSU, I also eagerly signed up for everything on campus provided there was a freebie, especially a free T-shirt. Soon my wardrobe was filled with white T-shirts that proclaimed the greatness of Wells Fargo Bank, or why you needed Mastercard for the things that you could in fact buy. With my coupon-bought shampoo and my free T-shirts, I felt more American and could put away my India-bought clothes.

The freebies extended beyond clothes. Every international student that came to America in the early nineties built their music collection through Columbia House and BMG, the mail-order music companies whose eagerly anticipated flyers would arrive with the other sale brochures in the mailbox. We had all figured out the optimal formula: you got the first ten to fifteen CDs free or for a mere penny, bought the remaining five at full price to complete one's membership commitment, and then promptly canceled the membership. This averaged out to four dollars a CD which, in the days before ninety-nine-cent downloads, was a steal. It was a business strategy that embodied American entrepreneurship and suited the frugal habits of an international student. And the repertoire was always the same: Aerosmith, the Allman Brothers Band, the Eagles, Air Supply, and all other manner of classic American rock. To diversify our

CD collection, Vikram and I obtained separate memberships and selected different CDs.

But these were small, temporary solutions to building an American-style life. We needed more resources. It was becoming difficult to get by on our small stipends and the little bit of extra money that Vikram was making through tutoring students like Mary. Unlike my American classmates who could go off and do whatever they needed to support themselves, I couldn't just go out and get a job or even flip burgers if I wanted. As an international student, I was bound to my teaching assistantship as my only source of income, and the immigration rules did not permit me to earn money through any off-campus jobs. By then, my assistantship had increased from the initial $740 per month to the princely sum of $1,000 per month. But even with the increase my annual income was just barely above the poverty line of $7,900.

SOON, AN OPPORTUNITY presented itself. Dr. Bishop called me to his office.

"Are you willing to teach an off-campus class at IBM in my place?" he asked.

"I'll do it," I said, leaping at the opportunity to have some extra income. It was a win-win situation for both of us. By now it was evident to me that the more senior and tenured professors like Dr. Bishop were, the less they were expected to or wanted to teach. This was especially true at large research universities in the US, where the success of professors was assessed based on how much they published and the size of the grants they brought in, not how well they taught. Instead, temporary, non-tenure-track instructors—which included graduate teaching assistants—taught most classes on US campuses, a practice that had increased over time. Since the early 1980s, the number of universities employing international teaching assistants to teach undergraduate courses had also increased, and most of the teaching of such courses was left to graduate students like me— despite the fact that we had not received any training in how to be effective teachers.

My lack of teaching experience was compounded by being an international teaching assistant. I now understood the suspicion with which those Introduction to Psychology 101 students had viewed me on my first day as a teaching assistant. Although I was one of the few international students in my entire department, many of the lower-level undergraduate courses in the science and engineering departments were being taught by Indian and Chinese international students, who made up half of all graduate students in these fields, most of them with teaching or research assistantships.

Unfortunately, many of the American students struggled to understand what these foreign-born assistants were saying. Soon students and parents began to complain, leading many US states to pass bills that required international teaching assistants to demonstrate their ability to be understood by their American students. A 2005 bill in the North Dakota legislature stated that if a student complained in writing that his or her instructor did not "speak English clearly and with good pronunciation," that student would then be entitled to withdraw from the class with no academic or financial penalty and would even get a refund. And if 10 percent of the students in a class came forward with such complaints, the university would be obliged to move the instructor into a "nonteaching position," which meant that the class instructor would lose the assistant.

Many American institutions now offer international graduate students intensive training in speaking American English so that they can succeed as teachers in classrooms and labs, with some international students spending up to two hours a day and a full year in training with the goal of being understood by their American students.

But some of the problem also had to do with tolerating difference. I overheard young American students mimicking the foreign teaching assistants, undulating their heads to imitate the stereotypical Indian head roll, and replacing an "r" with an "l" when imitating their Chinese assistants. Was it really so hard to understand a different accent? Did Americans ever wonder or worry about whether their English would be understood when they traveled abroad? For my part, I continued to struggle with the Southern American accents I heard all around me in North Carolina.

I HAD NOW been driving for some months, but I was still too nervous to drive on an interstate highway. To get to the class I was to teach at IBM in place of Dr. Bishop, my plan was to take a shuttle service that connected the cities in the so-called Research Triangle—Raleigh, Durham, and Chapel Hill—and the three large universities they housed. On the long ride over, I reviewed my notes and overhead slides for the first lecture. It was the same Introduction to Applied Psychology class that I'd already taught as a graduate assistant at NC State, but everything else about this new class was different.

The students were all adults employed at the large IBM facility in Research Triangle Park. They had never received a college education and were now taking courses as part of a continuing education program. They were all white, all older, and probably all Southerners. I had never felt more foreign, and the nervous feeling I had experienced on my first day on campus suddenly came rushing back. I had deliberately dressed in a way that made me appear older than my twenty-two years, pulling my one formal dress out from the back of the closet. I applied full makeup as I was discovering that a made-up finish made me look older and sophisticated.

But none of this helped when it came to my Indian-accented English.

"Excuse me, miss."

I turned around from the chalkboard. It was the day of the first class, and I had given everyone a break for ten minutes halfway through. Mr. Grant must have been about fifty or so and, up close, I could see the wrinkling of the skin on his neck and the redness of his scalp where the hair had thinned.

"May I borrow that piece of chalk for a second?" I handed him the chalk. He painstakingly wrote a single word on the board and then handed the chalk back to me.

"Laboratory," I said, pronouncing it in five syllables the way I'd learned back in India.

"No, lab-ra-tory. You see, we say lab-ra-tory here," he said kindly. There was nothing offensive about his gesture; it was well-meaning. But I felt embarrassed and angry, and my face flushed. I thought of all the corrections I had endured since arriving in the US: the constant questioning of my accent, the self-doubt over whether I could in fact speak the language that had been my language since birth. It felt like an unending struggle to fit in when I stubbornly clung to my accent and didn't Americanize. I was also tiring of cracking jokes when an American would say to me, "I like your accent," and I would quip, "And I like yours."

No statement frustrated me more than, "Oh, you speak such good English!" as if this were a terrific accomplishment when, in fact, I thought, spoke, and emoted in English and had done so since childhood. These statements reflected the ignorance of Americans about the colonial history of India and that English is the only truly common language in a nation of twenty-two languages and dialects.

But I also realized that my struggles with having Americans see me as a native English speaker were also wrapped up in my own complicated relationship with English and, more importantly, with Hindi.

Growing up, I spoke only in English with both my parents; I read English books, and all my early literary influences were drawn from England. It was a childhood steeped in Enid Blyton and James Herriot books, generously made available by British Council libraries which were the only lending libraries in India. The primacy of English was never questioned, and the language and ways of those who brought it to India was what we all aspired to. I don't recall having ever spoken a word of Hindi to either of my parents, but I learned it nonetheless in school and subliminally, since I was surrounded by it. Although Hindi was the vernacular of the house help, the vegetable hawkers, and the shopkeepers, it was understood that at home we would all speak with each other in English, and in the "Queen's English," no less.

I also understood Punjabi, which was my family's original

language, but never felt comfortable enough to speak it, even though both my parents conversed with my grandparents in a mix of Punjabi, Hindi, and English. It seemed that with each generation, we were moving away from our linguistic roots and toward an existence defined by an Anglicized culture—in our language, in our food, in our books, and even in our aspirations. It was not unusual for someone like me, from an upper-middle-class family in India, to be educated in an "English-medium" school, to read Western literature, to dress in Western clothes, and then to eventually aspire to the best education of all—a degree from the UK or the US.

Language was much more than just a means to communicate. In India, the way one spoke English said everything about where that person came from, what their family background was, where they had studied, and—in short—where they stood in the hierarchy of Indian society. In Sanawar, even though we had the requisite classes in Hindi and Sanskrit, we were dissuaded from speaking Hindi and it was considered cool to say, "Oh, my Hindi is very bad!" Hindi was reserved by the boys for choice profanities, which somehow seemed cruder when uttered in a language that wasn't English. English was the language of refinement, while Hindi was the language reserved for something less civil and almost shameful. We mocked those teachers who couldn't pronounce certain English words correctly, or who mangled the language. There was the perennial joke about the teacher who instructed a student to open the windows of the classroom to "let the climate in," when all he wanted was some fresh air. Or, worse yet, the commerce teacher who created a scandal when he said, "You love commerce, and I will make love to you," when what he meant was that he would love it if his students grew to love the subject he cared so deeply about.

As I struggled to have my English understood in America, a funny thing happened: I found myself speaking in Hindi more often than I had ever done before. Most of my Indian friends in North Carolina were from different corners of India and spoke different Indian languages; English was the only language many of us had in common. But with those who did speak fluent Hindi, I found myself using it more and more. It became our own special and secret language when in public, while also providing a link to India and home.

Now, as Mr. Grant stood before me, chalk in hand, I was tempted to apologize for my accent, and to offer to correct my pronunciation. But I decided to take a different approach this time.

"Mr. Grant, thank you for your comment. You see, in India we speak English differently and pronounce words differently. So just like you wouldn't expect someone from New Zealand to change the way they speak, you shouldn't expect me to change the way I speak. But if there's a word you don't understand, I'm happy to repeat it and spell it out."

There, I had said it. That wouldn't have happened a few months ago.

"Uh, sure," he said, looking a bit surprised, and then shrugged and walked away.

When I stepped out of the IBM building, I saw our small white Justy in the parking lot; Vikram had arrived to pick me up after my class. The stress from the day began to slip away, and I was silent during the drive back to Raleigh. My throat hurt from teaching two back-to-back classes that day, but I was also going over the events of the day in my head. I needed the money from the IBM class, but it was a heavy price to pay. I was conscious of every word that emerged from my mouth, and I felt so different from the students I was supposed to teach.

When we got home, Vikram quickly assembled some pizza crusts with sauce, cheese, and vegetables, and put them in the oven. I turned on the TV to watch *NYPD Blue*. This became our Tuesday evening routine: pick-up from IBM, the quiet drive back, homemade pizza, and the distraction of a gritty New York police drama.

MOST OF THE international students in Glendale Village shared bedrooms and were packed into cramped apartments like sardines—the only way to survive on international student teaching or research assistantships. Some, like my neighbor Ravi, just couldn't deal with it, and sought refuge in other ways. He would speak at length with his long-distance girlfriend in Bombay and ended up squandering all his money on those calls. There was a rumor that his father had to sell off his property in Bombay to pay off Ravi's mounting debt in the US.

What international students could afford to spend on food often affected what they ate. Having discovered the lure of the two-for-one burger and the satisfaction of a cheap but filling meal, many international students would stream into the McDonald's on Hillsboro Street, situated conveniently across from the NC State campus. Even Indian students who were Hindus and for whom beef was taboo didn't think twice about chomping down on a juicy patty, a transgression that their parents would never discover. I suppose I managed to avoid the descent into fast and cheap American food as I was busy saving every penny I could, so that even a one-dollar cheeseburger seemed like an unnecessary luxury.

But not all international students were struggling. Some Turkish students seemed to be awash in funds: not only were they supported on full scholarships by the Turkish government but they had managed to secure funding from NC State as well. Elif was one such student. She managed to get admission into the doctoral program in physics at NC State even though she struggled with fundamental concepts that didn't require a degree in physics. She was one of almost 8,200 Turkish students in the US that year, many of whom were on their government's study-abroad scholarship program which, since the 1920s, aimed to send the smartest Turkish graduate students abroad to acquire advanced knowledge and training.

While the rest of us saved every dollar, Elif shopped in expensive department stores, bought Lancome makeup instead of drugstore-bought Revlon products, and loaded up on designer clothes and perfumes for her family back home. But her relative affluence—and that of other international students in her shoes —came at a price. Given the substantial investment the Turkish government was making in sending its students abroad, it wanted them back: male students were required to serve in the Turkish military for a brief period after their studies, and the women were required to teach at either remote or urban universities in their homeland.

I thought this a fair exchange, given how much the country had invested in these young men and women and how much it stood to lose if they simply didn't return. I wondered why India hadn't expected more from its IIT students, most of whom left

for the US after completing their undergraduate studies at one
of the IITs. Although they weren't coming to the US on scholarships from the Indian government, their elite education while at
IIT had been heavily subsidized by the government, and the level
of taxpayer resources invested in these world-class institutions
was disproportionate when compared to all other colleges and
universities in India. The Indian government was investing all its
money in educating these budding engineers, fully expecting
them to build India's postindependence science and technology
enterprise, and yet most of these newly minted IIT grads had
dreams of America in their eyes.

Meanwhile, students like me at Delhi University, who were
pursuing the lowly humanities and social sciences, didn't even
have access to the latest textbooks that we needed for our studies. There was just one college library in all of Delhi that contained the latest textbooks in all fields—the IIT-Delhi library.
The irony was not lost on me that the very institution that was
receiving the most resources to be world-class, to have state-of-
the-art buildings and facilities, to have the best and latest academic materials and books, was also one where this investment
was yielding the lowest returns for India.

Learning about Elif's generous funding got me thinking:
Were there other sources of support that I had not explored? I
began to spend long hours at the campus library and on the internet, searching for fellowships and scholarships for students
like me. What I discovered surprised me: there was a great deal
of funding available if only one knew where to look. While there
is no single estimate of all the possible scholarships available, the
Fulbright Commission estimates that there are over six hundred
American institutions that offer scholarships to international

students (beyond the teaching and research assistantships available through departments on campuses), and there are many more offered by nonprofit foundations and organizations. I narrowed my selection down to two: the World Bank's Robert McNamara Fellowship and the American Association of University Women's International Fellowship.

By then, I had had enough practice writing personal essays and marketing myself and my interests. I didn't get the World Bank scholarship, but I received a very generous fellowship from AAUW: $15,000 over two years. This addition to my modest graduate teaching assistantship felt like a windfall.

But I also felt the weight of the future successes that were expected of me: I was one of only forty-two women worldwide awarded the fellowship, and I was following in the footsteps of more than 3,600 women from over 150 countries that had received the fellowship since its founding in 1917. I had promised a lot in my fellowship application: I would continue my focus on girls' education; I would take my knowledge and skills back to India to change the lot of girls and women who weren't as fortunate as I. But would I be able to follow through on these lofty goals?

PART II

One's destination is never a place but a new way of seeing things.

—HENRY MILLER

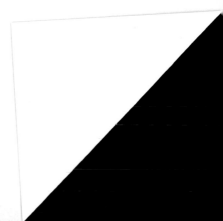

11

Foreign-Returned

I was on a plane, approaching Indira Gandhi International Airport in Delhi. Almost a year earlier, I had left for the US with Vikram in the middle of the night. Now it was daytime and I was returning by myself. Instead of the bright blue sky I had grown accustomed to in North Carolina, there was the dense smog and watery sun of Delhi. The dry heat of May in Delhi hit me as I left the chilled air of the terminal and stepped into the arrivals area, a heat so intense that even breathing felt difficult. Throngs of people jostled each other and craned their necks to catch a first glimpse of their visitors. Chauffeurs held up placards with scrawled names. I had waited and saved all year for this moment of arrival, of return. But it now felt loud and chaotic.

I spotted my father in the crowd. He looked leaner than before, his hair now completely gray. He embraced me tightly, almost with a sense of desperation, and said, "Long life Rajika, long life, Rajika," a mantra he had devised when I was a child and that he chanted each time he saw me. Then he went off to fetch the car. When he pulled up, I saw that he had neglected to remove the spare tire and junk from the already tiny car. How would we fit ourselves and so much luggage? He pushed away the boy who wanted to make a quick buck hauling the suitcases into the car. We finally managed to squeeze ourselves and every-thing into the minuscule car—my father and I, two international-sized suitcases, a small carry-on, and yes, the spare tire.

It was a long drive to my grandmother's home. Huge trucks and fancy cars with musical horns zipped around us while we lumbered on at a snail's pace. I didn't speak much during the drive, concentrating instead on all the familiar sights: the Mehrauli Highway, the Centaur Hotel, the Delhi Cantonment area, and Ridge Road. Finally, we turned left on the street that led up to the Bhandari house. I noticed for the first time that the street had no name. All these years I had instinctively located the street by the landmarks around it: the red brick exterior of a five-star hotel and the taxi stand at the corner. But my year in America, where every street had a name, had forced me to think of my sur-roundings in terms of cardinal directions: north, south, east, west.

We pulled up at the spot where my paternal grandparents' house had stood for over fifty years. But gone was the dilapidated house and in its place was a bright white, modern yet somewhat baroque four-story apartment building. A shiny black marble plate with gold lettering announced the number of the building, 4/11 East Patel Nagar. Eight families now lived one on top of the other on the very spot where my grandparents had begun to re-build their lives over fifty years ago after they had fled Pakistan as refugees. East Patel Nagar had become one of the largest refugee resettlement neighborhoods in Delhi. But pressured by greedy builders and the need for more money, most of the old Punjabi families on the street had one by one traded in their old homes and land for the modern buildings that now dominated the street.

Dadi opened the front door of the apartment. She looked as

frail and tiny as ever, a shrunken figure in her American duster coat and oversize glasses. It felt strange, as if I was visiting her in someone else's home. But despite the newness of the building on the outside, the inside of the apartment already seemed old and tired, with dust and grime everywhere.

I was going to share a bedroom with my grandmother, our two twin beds pushed together. That first night, I lay awake for a long time, sweating under the slow rotation of the ceiling fan, no longer used to the loud buzzing of India's aggressive mosquitoes. Raising the speed of a fan had been a battle with my father for many years: when I was a teenager, he would often sneak into my bedroom in the middle of the night to slow the blades' rotation. He was convinced that if a fan spun too fast, it would simply fall from the ceiling, slashing the body of whoever lay beneath it.

THE NEXT MORNING, I unpacked the gifts I had brought for my father, Dadi, and my uncle Kalyan, who also lived with them. If there was one thing my father always admired from America, it was sneakers. To him, running shoes epitomized all that was great about the country: the freedom of movement, speed, and the pursuit of exercise and sports. A pair of Nikes or Adidas were always his prized possession and he wore them all the time—with jeans, with tracksuits, and with a sports coat. He had ensured a steady supply of them over the past several years by purchasing them during his own trips abroad or receiving them as a gift from Uncle Satish. This time around, he had traced his foot on a piece of paper and sent it to me so that I could get him the right-sized shoes. For my grandmother I brought back almonds, which she promptly stored in her large wooden cupboard, along with the old purses and lace-edged handkerchiefs that were taken out for special occasions. She believed in the nourishing power of almonds: soak some each night and eat them the next morning, she always urged.

A few nights later, my father donned his new running shoes and a sports coat and off we went to a fancy gathering at the Imperial Hotel, an iconic colonial-era fixture with sparkling white buildings set amidst sprawling green lawns and towering palm trees. I knew that my father had probably wangled the invitation by picking up the phone and pestering the organizer of the event, Eyvah. He had done this my entire childhood, whether it was arguing about the price of an item in the market or repeatedly asking my school's headmaster for a scholarship. But despite my misgivings, I agreed to go along with him that evening because it had been several years since I'd had the opportunity to mingle with Delhi's bon ton and cultural elite, and I was curious.

Champagne was being served at the entrance to the ballroom. For my father, the main draw of such parties was the free-flowing liquor and the tables laden with food. His eyes gleamed as he spotted the champagne flutes. I held my breath, waiting for his characteristic nudge.

"*Beta*, be sure you have a glass or two of the champagne," he said, cocking his head in an obvious manner toward the waiter.

"I know," I hissed under my breath. I looked around quickly, hoping no one had seen our exchange. But he soon left me to my own defenses as he went off to schmooze and chat up young single women. I was relieved to be left by myself. My father had a habit of taking along young women to such events, and the last thing I wanted was to be mistaken for someone other than his daughter.

As expensive liquor flowed and waiters served delectable hors d'oeuvres, the cocktail party was in full swing. Women were dressed in jewel-toned silk saris or black cocktail dresses and looked terribly sophisticated, and yet quite a few of them were vacuous socialites. I felt gauche and superior all at once. For those few hours I could have forgotten that I was in India. Imported champagne and wine was being served in a country where the average fruit costs 30 rupees a kilo and where my grandmother's maid, Rosy, had to save for years to be able to afford a 300 rupees surgery to correct her long-failing eyesight. All the clichés about India were right before my eyes: the rich had gotten richer and the poor had remained where they were, even though the country seemed to be marching forward with all the obvious symbols of prosperity—ubiquitous cell phones, cool cafés, and world-class shopping malls.

I had never pondered these contradictions before moving to the US. Poverty was just something one lived with in India; it surrounded you wherever you turned, and the only way to live with it was to become inured to it. But being in the US for almost a year had given me a new vocabulary with which to understand a country like India, part of the "developing world" or "the third world." Back in Raleigh I had begun to take classes in developmental economics and read Amartya Sen, the Indian economist and Nobel laureate. For the first time, I began to consider issues like minimum wage and to reflect on India's large informal sector and underground economy, which included all the maids who worked in our homes, our drivers, our washerwomen, and our gardeners—the entire machinery on which our lives depended, but whose existence and livelihood hung on their employer's moods and goodwill, with no protections whatsoever.

I looked around the gathering, feeling out of place. But then I spotted two familiar faces—Sheela Bajpai and her husband, Kailash, who had been in boarding school with me. I walked over to them. The Sheela I had last seen in a prim school uniform was now transformed into a glamorous socialite in a black sequined sari. She seemed self-conscious and surprisingly tongue-tied, a far cry from the bossy girl I remembered from our school days. Kailash, on the other hand, looked old and bloated, nursing a tumbler of Scotch in his hand. My father came over and joined us.

"Papa, meet Sheela Bajpai and Kailash," I said, introducing them.

"Good evening." Kailash shook my father's hand and then turned to me. "Actually, she is Sheela Kumar and not Sheela Bajpai. She was Sheela Bajpai before marriage." It was a small matter, but I was nonetheless taken aback at this unabashed display of proprietary patriarchal behavior. I glanced at Sheela, but she had turned away. Plenty of women all over the world were still taking their husband's last names, but I was rankled by the way Kailash had reminded all of us—including Sheela—that she could no longer claim the identity she was born with.

I suddenly felt exhausted and walked away to a quiet spot. I knew it was none of my business, but the conversation with the Kumars had bothered me. In many communities in India, even a girl's first name was changed so as to completely erase the identity she was born with, replacing it with her husband and his family's identity. I had no intention of changing even my last name after marriage. The name issue—to change or not to change—was just one of the growing issues between Vikram and me, as a result of which he probably perceived me as a "feminazi" and I perceived him as being unnecessarily old-fashioned.

After spending ten days with my father in Delhi, I finally went home to Bhopal. Even though my parents had divorced when I was very young, home was always where my mother was, and Bhopal had been home now for twenty-five years for her. The sense of home had less to do about the city itself, for my mother herself was a transplant from Delhi, but it had to do with all that was familiar: the house, my childhood collection of books, the furniture, our dogs.

After their divorce, my father had moved from place to place, but my mother and our home had remained the one constant for me, an anchor, as I too had moved away, first to boarding school, then to Delhi for college, and then to the US. The constant separation and increasing distance seemed to have taken a toll on my mother: for the first time, I noticed the beginnings of gray streaks in her hair and the faint wrinkles when she smiled. It seemed as if she had aged in just the year that I had been away.

I DOZED AS Manju, the massage lady, pummeled me with her hands and droned on, sharing neighborhood gossip. She was a Muslim who had taken a Hindu name for reasons of social acceptability and went from house to house in the neighborhood to give massages at the rate of 40 rupees an hour, or less than a dollar. She kept falling asleep while massaging me. She had been up since 3:00 a.m. to cook and eat, since it was Ramadan and she was required to fast once daybreak came.

"Is this your *sasural*, your in-laws' home?" she asked.

"I'm not married," I replied, for what felt like the hundredth time on this trip.

"Really? I thought you would have at least a child or two by now," she opined. *Great,* I thought to myself, *this only gets better.* I asked her to drop the subject. She kept quiet for a short while but obviously couldn't control herself.

"Don't worry, you will get married soon. After all, you seem quite marriageable. Will you marry in America itself?"

From the neighborhood massage lady to the beauticians at the salon to my mother's well-meaning colleagues, everyone seemed preoccupied with my marital status. Had I made a good marriage? And if not, why not? These intrusive questions were followed by unsolicited advice: perhaps I should try losing weight, or perhaps young women these days had become too picky and set their sights too high. I just wanted to be home but, everywhere I turned, it seemed my very worthiness depended on whether or not I was married. Nobody asked me about what I was studying in the US, what my life was like in the US, or what my campus and friends were like. The constant questions increased my anxiety about why Vikram and I were still not married. The truth was that I no longer had any reasonable justifications to offer, and it was getting increasingly difficult to rationalize to myself and my family why we both continued to live in the gray, undefined zone of being engaged.

At cocktail parties, too, the conversation would take a familiar turn.

"Aren't you married?" asked Harish, a Punjabi gentleman I had known for many years who showed up at such parties with his demure wife and then proceeded to get totally drunk. I thought the superficial cocktail parties were a feature of the Delhi social scene, but Bhopal had its own version of such gatherings, with imported liquor and waiters who made the rounds with dainty finger foods.

"I'm not, Harish," I replied.

"Well, then you better hurry up! You're turning into a spinster, *yaar*," he said. That was a new one. I didn't realize that people still used the word "spinster." There was silence in the room and I felt embarrassed. On past occasions, Harish had made comments about my weight, my looks, and now this. Each time it happened, I would berate myself afterward for not stepping up and defending myself, for allowing him to speak to me in this insulting way, perhaps because I was a woman.

Growing up in India, it was not uncommon to have males that we knew—fathers, brothers, uncles, friends, classmates, boyfriends—comment freely on our appearances: the color of our skin, our weight. It was often couched as a joke, making it difficult to challenge, but it was a form of dismissiveness and ridicule. I don't ever recall a girl or a woman openly telling a man, however jokingly, that he was too fat, or too bald, or too old. America seemed so different in comparison; no man there had ever passed comments on my appearance, at least not to my face, except some of my Indian friends at NCSU.

I should have said something to Harish, should have put him in his place, but I once again lost my nerve. I got up and walked out of the living room and onto the lawns where the other guests were mingling. My friend and the evening's host, Saurabh, introduced me to an older gentleman who was his golf partner and a colonel in the army.

"Do you live here?" the colonel asked.

"No, I live in the US," I replied.

"Ah, okay," he said, nodding at me almost knowingly, a slow smile spreading across his face. "Are you married?"

I knew I shouldn't have been surprised, but there it was

again, though this time the intent of the question was quite different. The colonel was flirting with me, even though his elegant wife was almost within earshot. This was another, more seamy side to not being married: young Indian women who were single, unattached, and Westernized, especially if they actually lived in the West, were viewed as being "fast" and having loose morals. In the colonel's eyes, I probably embodied the stereotype of the single Indian female from America.

While I was being viewed as fast and available, I had been preoccupied with modesty, which was the litmus test for all my decisions prior to visiting India. How would I dress in India so as to not be perceived as being too Western? How short was too short for a hemline? Was a neckline too low? Shopping and packing for this first trip to India had begun almost two months earlier, as soon as I'd booked my ticket. I had separated my clothes into two piles: can be worn in India, cannot be worn in India. Could be worn before the male house help; could not be worn before them. There was the constant pressure of decorum and maintaining a sense of mutual respect and propriety, theirs as well as mine.

Between the larger Indian community that obsessed about my marital status and the sleazy older men, I was beginning to feel drained. I felt burdened by expectations, either of me as a woman, or as someone who was "foreign-returned."

Some of those expectations were connected to gift giving. Everyone back home expected to receive something from me, and what I got for them would be carefully assessed and then discussed, its merits weighed against other things that people had received from overseas. I felt like an Indian Santa Claus from America. I'd found myself struggling to figure out what to get for whom and, more importantly, how to leverage all the buy-one-get-one-free deals and the coupons so that I could bring something for everyone. It was the early nineties, when foreign goods were still not easily available in the Indian market and gifts from abroad were coveted, from Head and Shoulders shampoo and bras for women to underarm deodorant and chocolates. I remembered how Uncle Satish had brought gifts for everyone, and I now understood his gift-giving dilemma. The items might have changed over time between his visits and mine, but the allure of foreign things remained.

The simple fact that I lived abroad, in the affluent West, led my relatives to believe that I was rich. They all expected me to drive a sleek new car, own a large TV, and have all the material trappings of the American life that they imagined. My aunt asked my mother to see if I could get her a Chanel bag; I instead gifted her a black quilted toilet bag with some makeup, both of which had been free gifts with another purchase. For the house help, I carried some of the free T-shirts I had received on campus. Ravi, our housekeeper, was fascinated by the dollar. He wanted nothing more than to have a few dollars, even though he wouldn't be able to exchange them easily. But the expectations of me weren't always about material things: our neighbors wanted me to help with their child's admission to American colleges. My opportunity to go abroad had opened the door to more opportunities for them, albeit vicariously.

TWO MONTHS OF my summer break had flown by, and it was time to return to the US. My mother and I embarked on a shopping and packing frenzy like the one when I had first left for America. I had two suitcases I could fill to capacity. I bought block-print bedspreads, handicrafts, clothes, shawls, and books by Indian authors that weren't available in the US. There were frequent trips to the bazaar to buy sweet and savory snacks. Homemade pickles were carefully sealed into jars wrapped tightly with tape lest the oil escape. The flavors of home would last at least a few months after my return.

On the flight back to the US, I kept imagining how my mother would have felt when she returned to Bhopal and to an empty house after seeing me off. "Be sure you don't forget something," my mother had said.

I had packed and brought away every item of mine, and there wouldn't be a single trace of my presence from the summer. And yet I knew there would be reminders of my presence everywhere: my mother would remember me from that summer sitting for hours at the computer, reading my book on the hammock, playing with Toby, our dog.

As for me, even though I had flown for thirty-six hours through three different time zones, I felt that it had taken but an instant to transport me from home to Raleigh, where I was once again a spectator to my mother's life in India rather than a participant in it. When I made that first phone call home to let her know that I had reached Raleigh safely, I wondered which phone she was cradling to her ear—the white one by her bedside or the black cordless one? Both our voices were tremulous on that first of many long-distance phone calls to come.

BY THE TIME I had visited India that summer, I had been away for only ten months, yet everyone expected that I would have somehow changed in the short time I was away.

"You haven't changed at all! You haven't acquired an American accent!" they remarked, wonderingly.

I might not have changed on the outside—I still spoke with my Indian English accent, I still wore the Indian clothes I loved —but I was beginning to change on the inside.

Some of the changes were not for the better. I felt a sense of borrowed superiority through my association with America, and the attitudes that I had seen amongst many Americans toward poorer countries were slowly making their way into my perceptions and behavior. I caught myself looking down on many things in India, assessing everything by a new standard set by America.

The interiors of Indian homes felt dark and gloomy, made worse by the low voltage and constant fluctuation in electricity. The lights weren't bright enough and were dim and depressing compared to the lights in my apartment in Raleigh. Why did we use fluorescent tube lights everywhere in India, exposed, white, and clinical? Why had I never noticed the dirty streaks that the heavy monsoon left behind on buildings that had just been whitewashed? Was it the ravages of the extreme Indian climate, first the heat and then the torrential monsoon, that made even new buildings look gray and tired in no time? Was it really possible for dirt to accumulate so quickly? I had grown up comfortably middle-class, but now everything in India seemed shabby in comparison to what I had seen in the US.

I also realized on the trip back home that I was becoming intolerant and unaccepting of so much about my Indian roots and culture. It was easier to reflect on the inequities of India when I was away from there and distanced in a detached way— an observer looking in, with the objectivity of the outsider but the experience of an insider. I had lived every bit of what I was now observing from the outside, whether it was the invisible daily shackles of being female, or the desirability of being light-skinned, or the good fortune of speaking English with the right accent. To understand the contradictions of my country, its dirty secrets, its racism, its sexism, I'd had to leave home, which allowed me both to learn about the unfamiliar and to look at the familiar with a fresh perspective. It was as if I was seeing my city and country from high above, each nook and cranny exposed as never before.

12

Foreign and Female: A Complex Calculation

I stood in front of the mirror and tugged at my new gym shorts so that they would cover more of my upper thighs. The free T-shirt I'd acquired when signing up for a Mastercard was long enough to cover my hips. While I had worn shorts before—our games kit in Sanawar was a pair of skorts, a tad more modest than shorts—wearing them outside of a sporting environment in India was rare. Feeling self-conscious, I headed to the NC State gym. I had never been to a gym before. It was my first experience of exercising in an enclosed building where the sole purpose was to play sports, pound away on exercise machines, and sweat, no matter what the weather. I thought everyone would stare at me, but the man at the entrance swiped my card without even looking my way. I wedged my way in between the tall basketball players who were entering the gym.

Over time, I became a regular there. To my surprise, I began to enjoy the rituals of the gym and the feeling of exhilaration after a good workout. I discovered step aerobics and weight machines and, for the first time, learned to distinguish my deltoids from my pectorals. I began feeling a sense of strength that went beyond my muscles. As a college student in Delhi, it had been impossible for me to even jog down a street without inviting unwanted attention, yet here men and women were exercising alongside each other, the men oblivious to the women in their scanty sports bras and shorts.

But while I was getting used to being in a common space with men and women, all of us huffing and puffing and sweating in unison, I struggled with the most gender-segregated place of all—the women's locker room. I was shocked that women stripped in front of each other as if it were the most natural thing in the world, and I thought back to the European exchange students in Sanawar who had bared their bodies with the same insouciance. As for me, I sought out the shower stall in the locker room, lugging my clothes with me, feeling conscious for being clothed rather than unclothed. It was like being at a nudist beach in clothes.

The ease with which American women and men exposed their bodies extended far beyond the locker room. Even when the temperature had barely risen to seventy degrees, the main meadow of the NC State campus would be covered with bare bodies strewn around like confetti, legs splayed to achieve the perfect tan. In India, women's legs were always covered—although, on the other hand, most Western women were baffled at how Indian women revealed their midriffs in saris and short blouses, big tummies and rolls of back fat notwithstanding. Of course, the one body part that both cultures coveted and therefore covered were breasts.

The American worship of the sun also ran counter to what we Indians had grown up with. Our entire focus was on protecting and shielding ourselves from the sun. During peak summer afternoons, we would all huddle inside the deep and dark recesses of the innermost bedroom in my grandparents' home in Delhi. There, we would feast on sweet, juicy mangoes kept by the bed in an icy pail. Everyone remained indoors, and the only brave ones outside were the vegetable and fruit hawkers with their carts and the ice-cream wallah.

But there was another reason for avoiding the sun. The sun darkened the skin and to be fair and light-skinned, as I was, was to have a ticket to everything. Face creams like Fair and Lovely abounded, as did the use of bleach for facials. Fairness epitomized beauty even if a person's other features were unremarkable. Mothers urged their daughters to shield themselves from the sun. My father was obsessed with it too. "Wear a hat," he urged, in his monthly letters to me from India. I had been raised to believe that my fair skin was one of my most important attributes.

WHILE WE WERE living at the postgraduate women's hostel at the University of Delhi campus, my friend Radhika and I had made a pact to start jogging in the early morning. But we gave up just three days into our regimen, not because of a lack of resolve, but because groups of young men had begun to chase us on scooters, laughing and catcalling. We had done nothing to invite the "eve-teasing," a coy term for such harassment. Our bodies were fully covered in long, baggy tracksuits. But I was used to the entitlement that Indian males seemed to have over girls and women, stripping us with their bold gaze—on the streets, on trains and buses, in the market. Everywhere.

As college girls, we partook in social activities that were probably rites of passage for urban youth in any other large city elsewhere in the world. We lingered over tall glasses of cold coffee in cafés, saved money to dine at restaurants, and occasionally danced the night away to the latest hits from the eighties in Delhi's discos. But with one ground rule: we always needed to be escorted, to have the protection of a man, be it a father, brother, or boyfriend. The unspoken message was that male predators were everywhere.

But sometimes the predators were in our own homes. They included real uncles, honorary uncles, male servants, drivers, teachers, tutors. When I was fifteen, my mother and I visited the beautiful Kashmir valley for the first time, accompanying my mother's friend Rupa Aunty and her daughter and son. Rupa was well-connected, and so on our arrival, we stayed at the home of Mr. Mansoor Khan, a local politician whom she knew. That first evening we were all catching up on our rest after the long journey from Delhi. Rupa Aunty, Tanya, and Dhruv were in their room unpacking, as was my mother. I was in the sitting room watching some TV, when Mr. Khan walked in to fix himself a drink from the bar cart in the corner of the room.

"*Beta*, what class are you in?" he asked.

"Tenth, Uncle," I replied.

"Okay. Are you liking Kashmir?"

I nodded. He was now stirring his drink and I hoped he would leave and that the polite, inane conversation would end soon. But he instead settled himself across the room in an overstuffed armchair and began to read a newspaper. I went back to watching the TV.

He got up a few minutes later to leave the room. As he passed me, he reached out and squeezed my breast. I sat still in shock. Questions ran through my head: Could I have imagined it? Was it an accidental brush of the hand? Surely someone as respectable as he couldn't do something as awful as this. But my gut told me that this was different and deliberate.

I left the sitting room and rushed to tell my mother. It was a horrible scene. My mother, livid and fierce, stormed into Rupa Aunty's room to tell her what had happened. And then she confronted Mr. Khan, who feigned innocence. It was the word of an older, respectable gentleman against that of an unreliable fifteen-year-old girl. Rupa Aunty couldn't believe that her friend could have done something so awful.

My mother asked me to pack my bags, and then she made a couple of phone calls. Luckily for us, she knew one other person in Srinagar. He was with the local police and assured her that he would be able to help. A couple of hours later, his car pulled up outside the politician's house, and we left after a huge fight between my mother and Rupa Aunty.

I could tell that my mother was very anxious—a single woman traveling alone with a young daughter was a ready target anywhere in India, but especially in a remote part of the country. Could we even trust the police officer? We were fleeing one man's shelter for another's. The next morning, we abandoned our holiday and returned home.

Girls like me in India had been raised to always be suspicious of the opposite sex, and this culture of fear pervaded everything: don't go there alone; don't talk to strangers; don't climb the tree; don't go near the stove. After the episode in Kashmir, I learned to be even more careful of all the gray, bespectacled, and respectable men in India whose avuncular mien concealed their wolfish behavior. I also threw away the favorite night suit I had been wearing that evening—a pajama set in navy-blue cotton with white polka dots and ruffles. I had done nothing wrong, but I somehow felt soiled.

Later, I learned to avoid the Delhi Transport Corporation (DTC) buses that plied between Delhi's main campus and other parts of the city, where nubile college girls invariably fell victim to lecherous glances, groping hands, and strange men rubbing up against them. My friends and I would travel in groups, seeking comfort in numbers, and yet there were cases like that of Monisha Verma, the sports captain of my college.

In August 1988, Monisha was returning from a sports practice and boarded a DTC bus that was vacant save for five men, including the driver and conductor. Spotting an opportunity, the five men tried to assault her, but Monisha—a physically strong sportswoman—managed to kick and fight them off and then leapt off the moving bus. The culprits were arrested five days later and a court case ensued. It was the worst sexual assault case of my college years, bringing the entire University of Delhi to a standstill as students staged sit-ins or *dharnas* to protest the rampant sexual harassment and assault of women. In 1990, Monisha became the first civilian woman in India to be awarded the Shaurya Chakra Award for bravery for showing her courage in such a situation.

What happened with Monisha was what could happen if one ventured outside the college campus. But one didn't have to veer far from the campus to be a victim to constant male scrutiny. Because my college was a women's college, it was entitled to "special protection" by the police, ostensibly to protect us from sex crimes and eve-teasing. But it was these same police officers—all of them men—who would huddle in their Maruti police vans and ogle at the women entering or leaving the college gates. And then there was the lone ranger who for days would appear across the street from the college gate, and then pleasure himself in full view of the women students. The policemen looked on, laughed, and did nothing.

The situation got even worse over time: twenty-five years later—a whole quarter century after the Monisha Verma case—an almost eerie replay also involved a bus and five men. On the night of December 16, 2012, Jyoti Singh—or "Nirbhaya," the fearless one, as she came to be known—caught a screening of the latest film, *The Life of Pi*, with a friend and then headed home to her family. She was doing what any modern young woman in Delhi might do in the new and globalized India of multinational firms, employment opportunities, world-class multiplex cinemas, and a new generation of iPhone-toting young men and women who worked and played side by side. But what happened next instead reflected the centuries of misogyny and almost animalistic hatred toward girls and women in India, especially against the rising generation of modern Indian women. Nirbhaya was assaulted and gang-raped. The barbaric violence shocked India and the world and occupied headlines for months to come. The case convulsed the country, with student and citizen protests occurring all over India, Nepal, Pakistan, Bangladesh, Sri Lanka, and even France and leading to the passage of stringent new laws in India.

Such things don't happen only in societies like India. Just a few months before the attack on Nirbhaya, a sixteen-year-old American teenager in the midwestern town of Steubenville, Ohio, was repeatedly raped during the course of the evening by two high school boys. While the world reacted with horror at the details of the Delhi bus gang rape, the Ohio incident received very little attention and was dismissed as aberrant behavior by two jocks rather than the outcome of any sort of systemic misogyny or rape culture.

BY THE TIME I returned home to India to visit, I knew there was no perfect country for women, but I also knew that America was proving to be the better of the two countries for me. Back in Raleigh, I felt a sense of freedom I hadn't felt in India. I was driving and could go where I wanted; I could say what I wanted and wear what I wanted. I discarded the grandfather shirts I had carried with me from India and that I had routinely worn to disguise my body. My posture was changing in America: I began to walk straighter, no longer feeling compelled to hide my large chest or to disappear into myself.

Men no longer gawked at me; in fact, I could have been invisible. At one level, it was unnerving because I suddenly felt unnoticed by the opposite sex: in India, my light skin had been enough to attract a great deal of welcome and unwelcome attention. Now, nobody cared. My newfound invisibility also brought with it a sense of safety. I wasn't constantly looking over my shoulder or keeping my elbows at the ready to defend myself and ward off a roving hand in a crowded bus.

But despite these obvious freedoms, I was beginning to notice the subtle disparities between women and men. I had always regarded America to be a land of access and equity, where women were equals and had freedoms that were unimaginable to me back in India. But as I continued to dig deeper, I was learning that the obvious and visible expressions of being able to choose—the freedom of movement, the freedom of dress, the freedom of speech—were often just that, external and at times superficial. They didn't necessarily translate into complete equality in the more unseen parts of American life.

I first realized this while working at a program offered through the North Carolina State Department of Health and Human Services that provided services for violent and severely disturbed children and youth. It hadn't been easy to get this job. I wanted work experience and desperately needed the money. I knew I had the smarts and had the time available, since all my classes were over; after five years of coursework, all I had to do was write my doctoral dissertation.

I would need to do something more to get by—to make the rules of the system work for me. I began to closely examine what exactly I could and could not do on my F-1 student visa. That's when I discovered NC State's cooperative extension program which, through its statewide programs, had an opening for an evaluation associate with the youth program. I was eligible to be hired for the role because the position was offered through NC State, and I would be paid directly by the university, which meant that I would not violate any of the terms of my visa.

Once I began working with the youth program, I had my first taste of financial freedom. I could live without having to count each dollar, without clipping buy-one-get-one-free coupons each weekend, and could use the heat without worrying about the electricity bill. I settled quickly into the work, eager to apply my knowledge of numbers and statistics to understanding the data gathered on the five hundred youths who were part of the program.

My office mates were Melanie Harris, a self-declared rocker chick, and Ralph, who exuded a cocky air and, with his wavy hair and good looks, resembled tennis pro Pete Sampras. Our small research team was led by Jose Martinez, who was originally from Cuba.

One afternoon as I sat entering data into a spreadsheet, Ralph turned to me and asked, "How much do you make?"

"Fifteen dollars an hour. You?" I wondered why he had asked. We were both hired at the same level for identical positions, so he should know what I made. I asked him the question back more out of politeness and boredom than genuine interest.

"Really? They offered me seventeen dollars an hour." I detected a smug expression on his face as he turned back to his computer, leaned back in his chair, and twirled a pencil in his fingers.

It was my turn to be surprised. Hadn't they advertised two identical positions, and hadn't I, in fact, joined a few months before Ralph? And I was well on my way to receiving my doctoral degree so, all told, I had more knowledge and experience than him. But the powers that be who had hired both of us apparently didn't think so.

I tried to put it out of my mind, but it wouldn't go away. The mental math began. It was a difference of two dollars an hour, which seemed small until one began to add it up. Two dollars times twenty-five hours per week was fifty dollars per week. Fifty dollars per week amounted to a total of $200 per month less that I was making than Ralph. I realized that there was so much I could do with that money. In one month alone, I could have afforded two nice business suits from Macy's instead of making do with the tasteful but cheap separates bought at Marshalls. In five months, the extra money would total the cost of a round-trip ticket to India.

I told Melanie about it. "You should forget about it. Ralph's a jerk anyway," was her assessment. But I couldn't forget about it. The more I thought about it, the more unfair it seemed. Was it because I was a foreign student, I wondered, or worse yet, a foreign student and a woman?

I decided to bring it up with Susan Dietrich, the director of the extension program where I went every two weeks to pick up my paycheck. She was in her office the day I went to pick up the check. I didn't have an appointment but took a chance and knocked on her door.

"Hi, may I help you?" She looked up from her computer and smiled.

"Hi, there's something I wanted to talk to you about and I was wondering whether you had a few minutes," I said. I had been practicing these words for a few days now, but there was no good way to say it.

"So, you know Ralph, right? The guy who was hired for the other evaluation assistant position?" I said. She nodded, her smile slipping just a little.

"I found out the other day that he's being paid a bit differently than I am and I wondered what the reason might be." This time her smile disappeared completely, and she instead raised her eyebrows above the rim of her glasses.

"Why do you think he's being paid differently from you?"

"Because we talked about it and he told me," I said.

"Well, I really can't discuss people's salaries with you, it's confidential." She had now turned her gaze back to her computer instead of looking me straight in the eye. "What we pay people is based on many factors that include their education, experience, and so on . . . it's a complex calculation."

A complex calculation in which I had ended up at the losing end. There didn't seem to be anything more to discuss. I waited for a moment and there was an uncomfortable silence.

"Okay, thanks for explaining it to me," I said, and turned to walk out of the door.

"Rajika, one more thing," she called out to me. "You're new to the world of work, but let me give you one piece of advice. It's never, ever a good idea to discuss salaries with people."

Susan Dietrich's words stayed with me for a long time afterward. Over time, I discovered that I wasn't an exception but was caught in an insidious reality: women in the US regularly made less money than men for the same job. This "gender wage gap" existed everywhere, even in offices where most workers were women. It didn't affect just young women like me who were at the beginning of their careers, but also women who were established teachers, lawyers, and doctors. And the rift widened as we became more educated: women like me, with an advanced degree, could expect to make only 74 percent of what those like Ralph—our male peers—made.

It turned out that at US colleges and universities, too, women regularly earned less than men for the same type of role. I couldn't look at my professors the same way again. When I sat in class with my female professors, I wondered whether they were being paid less than Dr. Bishop even though they were just as senior and just as accomplished as he was. I also discovered that the gender wage gap was further tainted by the color of a woman's skin, or her origins: women of color fared the worst and made far less than white men. The gap for Asian women was smaller—eighty-five cents to a dollar—but it was a gap nonetheless. The final and least-understood piece of this puzzle was how being an immigrant, of being a foreigner and outsider, added to this accumulation of disadvantage over time.

As the gap widened, more and more women seemed to be falling into the abyss, yet most maintained a careful silence around the issue. After the episode at the North Carolina youth program, I too learned to keep my silence. I learned to do my research and to be smart about negotiations, but to never, ever make the fatal error of discussing what I made in relation to others, especially men. I also learned to keep my silence years later when, after months of desperately trying to relocate to California, I was finally offered a job with a research firm. But they made me a ridiculously low offer, well below industry standards. They knew I was desperate for the job, and that finding an employer who would be willing to sponsor me for a work visa meant that I would probably earn less than an equally qualified American.

But how much the complex calculation of being a woman and an international student affected me, I will never know. What I knew was that America was beginning to shape my understanding of what I could be both as an individual and as a woman. It was teaching me that my worth was not tied to the color of my skin, and forcing me to rethink my identity and to question where my sense of attractiveness lay, if not in my light skin. Yet it was also opening my eyes to the contradictions with which women live and the overt and hidden sexism that surrounds us—a reality that existed in both America and India.

13

The Best and Brightest

"Why did you choose to focus the study on China?" asked Dr. Jorge Garcia, one of my dissertation committee members.

It was the morning of my doctoral dissertation defense. My entire seventeen years of education in India and the US had led up to this moment, this culmination of sleepless nights, and poring over lines and lines of data that had resulted in a four-hundred-page research study. It was a test not just of my work but of who I was, what I knew and, most important, how far I had come in these six years.

"It's one of the world's fastest growing economies, and we're beginning to see dietary patterns in China similar to the West," I replied. For my doctoral dissertation I had chosen to study how mothers' education levels in Chinese households affected the eating behavior and nutritional status of a family.

Dr. Garcia nodded, exchanging a glance with the other four professors. "Thank you, please wait outside," he said.

I stepped outside the classroom and sat on a wooden bench as they decided my fate. Did they do this to every student? I wondered. Were they actually discussing the merits of my work, or perhaps the latest NC State basketball game?

I had completed my doctorate unusually quickly, taking just six years to complete both my master's and my doctoral degrees as compared to the average time of eight years. There was a common perception that international graduate students were brilliant—the best and the brightest drawn from all over the world—and that our academic outcomes were superior to those of our US counterparts. While some of this was true, it was also true that as international students we were held to impossibly high standards and stringent immigration regulations. The US immigration system tethered us to our classrooms and labs, allowing us little freedom to veer from a rigid timetable for study and graduation. Many of my American classmates began to take long breaks from their studies at around the three- to four-year mark in their graduate programs: some took on consultancies and part-time jobs; others simply decided it was all too much and took time off to mull over their dissertation topics. But I plodded on, because if I didn't, I risked falling out of legal status and would need to leave the US immediately. The stakes for completing on time were much higher for me than for my US-born peers.

I felt a hand on my shoulder. It was Vikram. He had left his class early to join me. After what felt like an interminable wait, my doctoral committee called me back into the room. Everyone smiled at me, which I took to be a good sign.

"Congratulations, Dr. Bhandari," said Dr. Bishop, "you did a great job." It was over, just like that. I had become the second person in my family to earn a doctoral degree from the US.

Vikram and I left Poe Hall and wandered out into th meadow behind the building. It was the same patch I had walked across six years ago, on my first when everything had seemed so foreign, so insurr now I felt a part of it. This is where I had grown up, where my mind had expanded to embrace so many possibilities, and where I felt limited only by my own imagination and the boundaries I set for myself.

But the day also felt strangely anti-climactic. I had often imagined this moment. Would I cry, would I shout with joy? But what I felt instead was relief and fatigue. Relief that it was all over except for a few cursory edits to the dissertation and the expensive printing. Fatigue at the long journey to get here and the equally tough road that lay ahead.

It was also my last day of work at the youth program. The team gathered during lunch to say farewell to me. Jose, who had the logical mind of a researcher but the soul of a poet, liked to begin our weekly meetings with the reading of a poem, and we all took turns each week bringing in a poem to share. That day it was my turn, and I had selected Rabindranath Tagore's classic, "Where the Mind Is Without Fear." I began to recite the poem slowly and deliberately.

> *Where the mind is without fear and the head is held high;*
> *Where knowledge is free;*
> *Where the world has not been broken up into fragments;*
> *By narrow domestic walls;*
> *Where words come out from the depth of truth;*
> *Where tireless striving stretches its arms towards perfection;*
> *Where the clear stream of reason has not lost its way;*

I felt a sudden rush of tears, and my vision clouded as I struggled to read the words. I was thirteen and back in Barne Hall at Sanawar, the smell of the tall pine trees drifting through the open windows as the deep voice of our headmaster, Dr. Shomie Das, rang out in the auditorium, reciting Tagore's poem only as a great orator could. We all listened, spellbound. That was home, a place I knew; a place my mother had known. There was a sense of belonging. But here at this youth program, in Raleigh, in North Carolina, I had no history, no background, no path behind me that I could turn back and look down, knowing that others before me had walked that road. It was only the here and now and the road that lay ahead. It was an existence without context, without heritage, without history.

I swallowed the wave of homesickness, tried to steady my voice, and pushed on, completing the poem.

Into the dreary desert sand of dead habit;
Where the mind is led forward by thee;
Into ever-widening thought and action;
Into that heaven of freedom, my Father, let my country awake.

The room was silent. I glanced up at Jose, hoping he hadn't noticed my watery eyes. He looked at me probingly, then cleared his throat and asked the group what was first on the agenda for the day.

VIKRAM AND I had not discussed it explicitly, but we'd made an unspoken decision that we wanted to stay on in the US for at least a few years. We had worked hard as students, and it seemed foolish to head back to India immediately when we could stay on for a while, earn some money, and test our newfound skills in the American workplace.

I wondered whether I was cheating the system. Six years ago, when I had stood sweating and nervous before the consular officer at the US Embassy in Delhi, he had asked me that fateful question: "Do you plan to return to India?" The F-1 student visa that I was applying for is what in consular speak is called a "single-intent" visa, which means that as an international student coming to the US, the burden was on me to prove to the consular officer that I intended to come to the US only to study and fully intended to return immediately after completing my education. Other countries, like the UK, Australia, and Canada, that attract international students in large numbers do not require them to make such promises.

I had looked the officer straight in the eye and said a confident "yes." And I had meant it. If it were not for Vikram, I might not even have been motivated enough to come to America. My family was back in India; I liked most things about India and had never known anything different, and I couldn't imagine why I wouldn't want to return to my own country.

But I had now experienced something different over the past six years. There were things about my life in America that I was beginning to enjoy and wasn't ready to give up just yet. I loved the freedom of zipping down a North Carolina country road, the wind in my hair; I liked the fact that I didn't have to worry about frequent power cuts or having a limited water supply; I liked the sanitized feeling of the streets in America; I liked that I didn't have to excuse my presence in a room full of men; and I liked that I could buy large containers of pasteurized and homogenized milk that didn't need frequent boiling to control the bacteria. In short, I liked the comforts of my first-world existence. I had weakened in my resistance to

America—I had become the proverbial fly trapped in American honey.

When I had first arrived as a student from India, most Americans would ask me: Do you plan to go back home? For some reason, they felt this was a perfectly appropriate way to start a conversation. Back then, when the pull of home and India was much stronger, I bristled at this line of questioning, responding with an emphatic "Yes, of course, I do plan to go back. Why wouldn't I?"

But I was no longer so sure. I had reached a crossroads. I could turn back and go home, or I could forge ahead along the path that lay ahead. America, it turned out, had choices and opportunities. After all, Starbucks, a brand that symbolized America, proclaimed that "happiness lay in choice," and Burger King encouraged all its consumers to "have a burger their way." Now I had to make a more consequential choice. It was for me to decide whether or not I wanted to seize the opportunity and live the American dream as millions had before me.

A FEW WEEKS after defending my dissertation, I made my way to the International Student Office on campus once again. This time, it was to find out more about applying for Optional Practical Training (OPT), a post-study work program for international students that allowed us to remain in the US for a year after our studies to gain some work experience. Where six years ago I had had to familiarize myself with all the terminology surrounding my F-1 student visa application, I now had to learn a whole new vocabulary, and the staff at the office patiently helped me navigate the latest immigration requirements: I-765, the application for my employment authorization; EAD, the Employment Authorization Document that would allow me to work on OPT; and "advance parole," which made me feel like a prisoner being granted a brief reprieve, but was actually a permit that would allow me to travel outside the US.

Ironically, for a country that celebrated instant gratification and had invented a "fast" version of everything, it took several weeks to compile the long list of documents needed for my application. Then there was a wait of a few weeks before I received a notification that my application had been received. This was followed by a wait of another three months before I received the actual OPT card that permitted me to work.

I began to apply for jobs. I knew by then that I wanted to work in the international field. I thought of my father's dream that I would join the United Nations. The work of the UN appealed to me, as did that of the World Bank. I looked at various websites, and at the classified ads in the *New York Times*. But after several months of submitting applications and queries and receiving no responses, it felt as if all my messages were going into a black hole. Unlike the graduates of business and technical programs who were courted by recruiters on campus, PhD graduates in the social sciences did not seem to be in demand.

Two things began to sink in. First, it seemed that Spanish, French, and Arabic were the only languages that mattered for UN and development jobs. I spoke none of these. I spoke Hindi, but that didn't count for much since India had never colonized any other country, which meant its language had never been spread across the globe.

The other issue had to do with my institution, NC State. When applying to universities in the US, I had not known anything about university rankings or the relative prestige of various institutions. My sole focus was on being as close to Vikram as possible; in addition to applying to NC State, I had applied to Duke and UNC Chapel Hill, which were both close to Raleigh. I didn't realize that NCSU was not very highly ranked for its social sciences, though it was well-known for its engineering program, which explained the large number of international students in the science and engineering programs but few international students in the social sciences. The IIT students back in India closely followed the rankings of American colleges and universities, even posting ranking lists on the bulletin boards in all the student hostels and carefully tracking the trajectories of their illustrious predecessors who had gone on to attend US institutions like MIT, Purdue, Cornell, and the University of Southern California.

Now I felt stuck.

"I don't know what to do," I mentioned to Farhad. I thought he might have some advice, since he had worked with the UN before going to graduate school.

"I hate to tell you this," he said, "but when we used to receive job applications at the UN, they used to go into two piles. One was the pile with applicants from big-name schools, and the other pile was everybody else."

I was a bit discouraged, but I kept applying to jobs, sometimes without even knowing exactly what the role entailed. It reminded me of the time my father had written painstakingly to university after university in the US, seeking admission for me. Now I was the one seeking help, not to come to America but to stay on. But there was no one to provide advice or to help me shape my cover letter and resume.

Then one day I got a call back for a job at a research center at the University of North Carolina, Chapel Hill, where I had applied for the job of an assistant director for evaluation. I had an interview with the executive director of the center, a portly gentleman by the name of Dr. Ben Winarno, an immigrant from Indonesia.

"Do you have work authorization?" he asked me.

"I do," I replied confidently, patting my purse in which the OPT card was secured. He didn't ask me much else but seemed pleased that I was Indian and a woman.

"You know, I find Indian women in saris so beautiful and elegant," he said, as I was making my way out of the office. I got a call from them later that day offering me the job, with a salary of $45,000. I was again left with the feeling that it was some combination of being female and being foreign that had got me the job, only that this time the combination had worked in my favor since Ben was himself an Asian immigrant and seemed to have an affinity for other Asians.

As for the salary, it was more money than I could imagine. I had made do with a lowly student stipend of $1,000 per month and would now draw a monthly salary of $3,750. Unlike many of my American classmates, I had zero debt and no student loans to pay off. Like many other Asians in the US, Indians had a household savings rate much higher than most Americans. We Indians knew how to be frugal and save, and that's what I planned to do.

VIKRAM MEANWHILE HAD been applying for jobs in California, home to Silicon Valley, a magnet for all science and engineering graduates. International students were particularly attracted by the allure of California's immigrant-driven start-ups, many being run by former international students who had arrived in the US soon after America's doors had reopened to global talent in the 1960s.

The late 1990s in California were the height of the dot-com boom, where ambition and opportunity came together under the California sun. The first California gold rush of the 1850s had attracted three hundred thousand gold seekers, merchants, and other immigrants from around the world, including thousands from Mexico, China, Britain, Australia, and France. Now there was a new wave of arrivals in California, pursuing their own version of American-style success and wealth. This time the dream was driven by knowledge and technology.

Where once there were citrus orchards in Santa Clara Valley, at one time the largest fruit production and packing region in the world, the rapid growth of industries and companies had now spawned tech parks—sprawling campuses of glass-fronted office buildings, large parking lots, and rows of carefully planted trees that were home to many of the world's largest high-tech corporations, including the headquarters of several Fortune 1000 businesses, and thousands of start-up companies.

The manicured transformation of the Santa Clara valley into a beacon for growth and innovation was accompanied by new migrants, most from China and India, and a spurt in subdivision-style living—cookie-cutter homes with middle-class amenities such as swimming pools and clubhouses. A common joke was that the most frequently spoken languages in Silicon Valley were Hindi and Telegu. If Glendale Village in Raleigh had once felt like a ghetto of struggling international students, these subdivisions in places like San Jose, Santa Clara, and Sunnyvale also felt like ghettos—albeit ones that were fancier enclaves of international students turned tech entrepreneurs. The international students who had once driven old secondhand cars had now acquired BMWs and Lexuses. They now partook in the all-American, Californian pursuits of wine tasting in Napa Valley, skiing at Yosemite, and hiking in Muir Woods.

Now Vikram was hoping to join these new migrants, while I stayed back in North Carolina. My plan was to follow him to California as soon as I could. I had exactly one year in which to find a job in California where an employer would be willing to sponsor me for an H-1B work visa. The clock was ticking.

14

A Temporary Arrangement

I left North Carolina for good and arrived in San Jose, California, on a bleak and chilly day in December 1999. All my belongings were once again contained in the two suitcases allowed by the airline and some boxes that I had shipped through the postal service. Everything else had been sold off or given away in North Carolina in anticipation of the new life that Vikram and I were to start in California. But Vikram wasn't there to receive me at the San Jose airport. He had gone away to India for three weeks.

A lot had happened in the past two months. It had been a schizophrenic existence. On the one hand, I had flown out to California frequently to interview for jobs and set up our new apartment. But on the other hand, the doubts and issues between Vikram and me had gradually come to a head. Marriage was no small undertaking, and we both knew that we couldn't move ahead while struggling with differences that made us question our compatibility. There was just too much that had been swept under the rug all these years and that was now staring us in the face. Just six weeks before the appointed date in December, we called off our wedding.

Afterward, many people asked me, "How could you remain

in a relationship for ten whole years and then discover suddenly that you're incompatible?" There is no clear answer to this question. Perhaps some relationships have more shades of gray than others, in which a lot is sensed but left unspoken. In any case what should have been apparent to Vikram and me in a year took a whole decade to fully reveal itself. It often came down to bad communication—the fodder for countless self-help books.

Vikram and I were also very young when we first met and, knowing what I now know about myself, about relationships, and about men, I firmly believe that most adults mature into being the people they will be only in their late twenties, and perhaps even later for men. After ten years of growing up together and finding our individual identities, Vikram and I had evolved in different directions as adults. He was devout and ritualistic when it came to religion, while I was an agnostic or at best a Hindu by culture if not by religious practice. Vikram believed in upholding long-held family traditions, while I tended to challenge the status quo. For him, the word of family elders was final, while I respected elders but evolved with the times, always questioning what seemed archaic or unreasonable. He appreciated smart and accomplished women (and came from a family of female superstars), but also expected them to dutifully follow familial and religious customs, while I was becoming increasingly liberal in my thinking—especially after coming to the US—and constantly questioned the ingrained traditions, practices, and expectations that shackled Indian women in invisible and entrenched ways.

In short, our differences were not of the superficial *When Harry Met Sally* variety, but rather were about fundamental beliefs that not only affected how we planned to live our lives, but also how we would raise our future children. All of which worried both of us enough to postpone the wedding.

But none of that stopped me from making the move to California. I agonized over the decision. What was the point of moving when what drew me to California in the first place—my ten-year relationship with Vikram—was hanging in the balance? My friends in Chapel Hill tried to stop me: stay here, they said, and if things fall apart completely, you will at least have your friends around you. But I still moved because I was not ready to let go. I believed that we would eventually work out our differences and set a new wedding date.

And now here I was, alone in California, because I couldn't bring myself to go to India in December, at precisely the time that our wedding would have taken place as originally planned. Our families had been devastated by our decision: my mother canceled the wedding banquet and lost her entire deposit for it; my carefully assembled trousseau and wedding outfit languished in suitcases. The shame of the canceled wedding was bad enough for my family, and I imagined it would cause them much more embarrassment if I showed up in India anyway. So I stayed back in North Carolina and instead planned my move to California.

But Vikram decided to go to India to see his family and attend his best friend's wedding. It was my decision to stay back, and yet I felt angry and resentful about his decision to go.

I made the best of my time. For several days in a row, I drove between Vikram's apartment in Santa Clara and the local post office to pick up the boxes that had arrived by mail, lifting and hauling cartons full of books and the vestiges of my life in North Carolina. Back at the apartment, I was surrounded by the boxes and all the new furniture I had carefully picked out during my visits to California over the past year, fully believing that this would be as much my home as Vikram's. This time around, we had not needed to rely on yard sales—we had come a long way from our days as struggling graduate students. We could afford to buy real furniture and even have it delivered. We picked out an elegant mahogany futon for the guest room; I framed paintings and photos for the bare walls; we bought a dining table with six chairs, large enough to accommodate family and friends who would undoubtedly visit once we were married.

For the second time over, I had created a home for the two of us, this one combining bits and pieces of our old life in North Carolina with symbols of our future life in California. Yet, now, surrounded by the remnants of my past and the reminders of a shaky future, I had never felt more alone in my life.

OVER THE PAST year, I had applied for several jobs in California, hoping that something would fall into place before my one-year OPT clock ran out. I met with employers during my many trips out west. But with no guidance from anyone on campus and with no contacts to rely on, many of my attempts were shots in the dark.

I interviewed for the role of a researcher with the San Francisco Unified School District and couldn't provide a solid answer to a question about culturally appropriate testing. The hiring manager—coincidentally an Indian woman with an American accent—looked at me with a mix of exasperation and pity. I never d back from her.

nother interview was with a well-known educational research firm in San Francisco. They flew me out for the interview, which went well. They knew I needed the job as my fiancé was already in the Bay Area, and that I needed them to sponsor me for my H-1B visa. They seemed unfazed at the prospect of hiring an international student and eventually made a job offer, but at a shockingly low salary. I suddenly felt that I was back at NC State, arguing with Susan Dietrich about why my salary was less than that of a male colleague with fewer qualifications than I. But this time it was different. The unusually low salary probably had to do with my immigration status. They knew that I really needed the job, for personal and legal reasons. I accepted the job and signed on the dotted line.

I heaved a sigh of relief: the job search was over and I could now focus on my upcoming move to California. I gave notice to Dr. Winarno. The research company had told me that their lawyer would be contacting me soon to begin the process of applying for my H-1B visa, but a few weeks passed and I didn't hear anything. Then came an email: "We apologize for any inconvenience, but we need to withdraw our job offer due to unexpected circumstances." I was stunned. Just like that, I no longer had the promise of a future job. In fact, it appeared I had no job at all, as I had already given notice at my job at Chapel Hill. Bill Schwartz, the director who had interviewed me, seemed sincere, with a frank and pleasant demeanor, which made this development even more surprising. There was no concrete reason given, no remorse, no understanding of the fact that for me it didn't mean just losing a job opportunity; it meant wrapping up my life in America and heading back to India, and probably without Vikram.

Angry and frustrated, I reached out to a pro-bono lawyer

who worked in employment law. I was told that most laws are stacked in favor of the employer. The reality is that employers can withdraw job offers with impunity right up until the day that a new hire reports to work, and that job candidates have few protections. I wrote a long letter to the president of the research company but never received a response. I wish the company had been honest enough to admit that hiring me would prove to be more of a complication than they were prepared to handle.

Meanwhile, Dr. Winarno turned out to be kinder than I had expected. He permitted me to stay on for longer at my job at the university. But my twelve-month clock was still ticking, and I had just a few months left to find a job in California.

About a month later, I interviewed for another job in Berkeley with MPR, an educational research firm. The interview for the research associate role went well, but I was terrified that what had happened with the company in San Francisco would repeat itself. But it didn't. I received an acceptable offer and a promise to sponsor me for an H-1B visa. The company lawyer reached out to me soon after and began the application process. For the second and final time, I gave my notice to Dr. Winarno in North Carolina. Two months later, in December 1999, I landed in Santa Clara, California, to begin the next chapter of my life in the US.

VIKRAM RETURNED FROM India a few weeks later, but I couldn't bring myself to speak to him about my sense of anger and abandonment. There was a wall of silence between us. Never one to initiate a difficult conversation, he pretended as if all was normal. I began to feel suffocated living under the same roof, engulfed in the silent anger and bitterness, and realized that I needed to find my own place. Vikram and I were still together, but we needed to be apart to work through our issues. Moreover, having moved cross-country after leaving my job in North Carolina, I felt dependent on him for everything—a roof over my head, my daily expenses, and a car.

I decided to move to the East Bay area, close to the location of my future office in downtown Berkeley. Each day, I borrowed Vikram's car, drove forty-eight miles north from Santa Clara up I-880 to the East Bay to look for apartments, then headed back before rush hour. I saw apartment after apartment and began to wonder whether I could afford anything on my own. The housing situation in the Bay Area was tight, and it seemed impossible that anyone other than Silicon Valley techies, flush with new money, could afford the sky-high rents. My head swam with names of all the "desirable" locations—Montclair, Piedmont, Claremont, Rockridge, Solano. For a newcomer to the area, there was no easy way to determine the exact location of these neighborhoods, for they were defined more by their proximity to all the symbols of gentrification—cafés, gourmet restaurants, and boutiques—rather than clear geographic boundaries.

I had never before been to an open house for a rental, with several anxious parties competing for the same tiny apartment. I soon discovered that "cozy" was a euphemism for tiny, and that an ad for "a beautiful cottage with a redwood deck" usually avoided mentioning the termites. If an apartment had a dishwasher, it didn't have off-street parking; if it had parking, it didn't have a balcony, and so on. To secure a place that met all my requirements, I would need to either revise my budget drastically or look for a roommate.

So I responded to an ad in Craigslist for a shared cottage in the small community of Kensington, bordering Berkeley. The house was rented by a woman named Rebecca who was looking for someone to share it with her. She showed Vikram and me around the house, and when I told her that I liked painting, she pointed out the small wooden shack at the end of the garden.

"That'll make a perfect studio," she said.

Rebecca was much older than me and seemed to be nice and affable. She was with a dance troupe and had the lissome build of a dancer. Her messy ash-blond hair was pulled into a loose bun and she dressed in masculine clothes: a dark button-down shirt with rolled-up sleeves atop a pair of dark cargo pants. Her feet were always encased in big black hiking boots that she kept on even inside the house.

I hadn't had a roommate since my graduate school days and hadn't planned on getting one when I moved to California, but for now the arrangement with Rebecca seemed perfect. I was in a new town, and it was comforting to live with someone older and with more knowledge of the area. It was also a nice neighborhood, close to transportation, and the house had a washer/dryer, parking, and a garden. I'd be sharing it with just one other person and would have to furnish just my room without worrying about the rest of the house. I still felt that this was a temporary arrangement and the fewer additional items I had to acquire the better, since Vikram and I already had everything we needed in his apartment in Santa Clara.

MY WAIT FOR the H-1B visa began. MPR's lawyer seemed adept and had filed all the necessary paperwork, but there was nothing she could do to hasten the process. Created in 1990, the H-1B nonimmigrant visa was intended to assist US employers who needed temporary workers. Unlike most temporary visa categories or the F-1 student visa, which is a "single-intent" visa, H-1B workers can intend both to work temporarily and to immigrate permanently at some future time. Since 1990 the number of H-1B visas available each year has fluctuated, averaging around sixty-five thousand, with an additional twenty thousand visas for international students with a graduate degree from a US institution.

In 1999, the year I applied for an H-1B, the Immigration Naturalization Service (INS) for the first time compiled information on who exactly these individuals were that were being approved for H-1B visas. That year, employers submitted three hundred thousand applications for H-1B visas, and most positions approved were related to IT and carried an average salary of $45,000. The median age was about twenty-eight years at the time of approval, and almost half were born in India, with the second-highest number from China. Many of the applicants were already in the United States as international students. Apart from not being in IT, I was the typical H-1B applicant that year: I was from India, already in the US as a student, and was twenty-eight.

While I waited for my H-1B to come through, the process for my future employer, MPR, was arduous and complex. First, as an employer who wished to hire an H-1B worker, the company had to work its way through numerous steps, beginning with the submission of a Labor Condition Application (LCA) to the US Department of Labor. The LCA is the employer's guarantee to the US government that the foreign worker is not displacing other workers in the company, and that they would be paid wages at par with domestic employees to not bring down the overall wages. Second, there was a significant financial and opportunity cost for employers like MPR to apply for an H-1B visa. Companies pay anywhere between $1,710 and $6,460 in fees to the US government for each visa, and this doesn't include legal fees. Then, it could take as long as four or five months for the visa to come through, resulting in stalled work and diminished productivity.

AS MY WAIT for the H-1B lengthened, I began to stay in my new home most of the time, scanning internet sites for updates and for some sign that my visa would come through soon. Living with Rebecca wasn't turning out to offer the comfortable stopgap arrangement I had hoped for. At times she seemed happy, a manic excitement in her eyes; at other times she raged angrily, often to herself or at her cat, a silent victim.

"Where the fuck is that bloody cat hiding? I'm going to kill that cat," she ranted one evening. But a couple of hours later, she was sitting before the TV, her feet propped on an ottoman, cooing to the cat curled up in her lap.

At other times she stomped around the house in her boots, always the boots. I suppose she took them off by her bedside, right before sleeping, but other than that they never came off. She fought with our neighbors because the light from their bedroom disturbed her, but she didn't want to put up any drapes to block the light.

I could tell that most things about me were also beginning to irritate Rebecca. I didn't wash the dishes right, I wasted too much water, and I didn't put out the recycling correctly. I followed her lead without argument because—even though I was a co-renter—I saw the place as her home, and also because I had begun to feel intimidated by her. I tried to not think too often about the array of saws and tools she stored in a tall cabinet in the kitchen and sharpened regularly. I began to feel I was living in my very own version of the diabolical thriller, *Single White Female*.

Then one day Rebecca couldn't contain her irritation with me anymore. I had left a used spoon in the sink after stirring my tea.

"How many times do I have to tell you to not leave even a single spoon in the sink?" she said, waving her hands in the air in exasperation. "All you do all day long is just sit around, lounging with your newspaper and sipping your silly cups of tea. How easy your life is. What do you do all day, huh? No job, nothing. You're useless! Such a damn loser." By now, she had moved closer to where I sat at the kitchen table.

"Rebecca, please . . . I was going to wash the spoon later."

"Rebecca, please," she mimicked me, rolling her eyes. "And what sort of accent is that anyway? You think you can speak English?" She mimicked me some more, adopting the hackneyed Apu accent.

I was stunned. I had now been in the US for eight years and, up until now, no American had ever openly mocked my accent or me for being a foreigner. Not my professors, not my American classmates at NC State, and not the IBM employees whom I had taught in Raleigh and who had struggled initially with my accent. If they thought such things, they never actually said them aloud to me.

Rebecca didn't know the details of my situation, but I could see why she saw me as a loser. It was now March, four months since I had a job or an income. I had moved to an area with a much higher cost of living and was quickly spending all my savings, with the prospect of going into debt suddenly seeming very real. I had no health insurance and couldn't see a doctor for any sort of preventive care. I was a "nonimmigrant alien" who in theory had a job, and yet didn't have one. I was a qualified professional but was forced to be unproductive. I had contributed my share to the American economy when working at the youth program in Raleigh and at UNC but couldn't claim any of the benefits to which Americans were entitled. I was in the country legally and yet felt as if my credibility and value were questioned each day. Stuck in this gray zone between a student and a worker, I felt I didn't have any identity at all.

The worst was that I had no ability to plan my time, as I had no way of knowing when the H-1B visa would come through. I longed to go home to India but couldn't leave the US without jeopardizing my H-1B application. During my past trips back home, I coveted each extra day of leave because it meant more time at home, in India. Now, I could have been in India all this time with my family and also saved $10,000 in living expenses. And the longing to go home wouldn't end with the arrival of the work permit: regardless of when I began work at MPR, it would be months before I could even think of taking a vacation.

I was not alone in my predicament. There were entire websites and bulletin boards devoted to the issues surrounding H-1Bs. Along with thousands of others, I checked these sites obsessively in an effort to predict when my H-1B might be approved. According to one estimate, it would be June by the time I would be able to begin work. That would be almost nine months after the company offered me the job, and almost seven months since I'd left my previous job in North Carolina. A distraught post on one of the threads read: "We don't have much more to lose—we have lost our jobs, our status and all our money. All we have left is hope."

The different locations of the INS processed H-1B applications at varying speeds, with the California branch suffering from the worst backlog: a process that might take a month at the Vermont INS could take four months at the California center. The reasons for the delays were never clear. In addition, the adjudicators who evaluated files varied in their judgment. At one service center, employers were required to provide a report from an independent agency that specialized in evaluating the credentials of foreign workers; other service centers did not care about this. Even within the service center that required these reports, there were differences of opinion amongst adjudicators about whether or not to accept reports from the same agency. At another center, an adjudicator familiar with the IT field didn't believe that IT occupations constituted specialty fields deserving of an H-1B visa. I wondered whether my application would end up being one of the lucky ones. All I could do was wait and watch and then go back to the drawing board if my visa was rejected.

I called the company's immigration lawyer repeatedly, but she felt helpless, too, and didn't know any more than did I about when the visa would come through. My hiring manager at MPR was supportive—after the experience with the research company where I was first to work and that had retracted its offer, I was worried that MPR might do the same since it was taking me so long to begin work for them. The delay in my H-1B visa—and countless others across the country—has a debilitating effect on the American economy. A company's work is held up indefinitely as it desperately waits for the new employee to begin work. In the end, everyone is the loser.

With my ten-year relationship with Vikram on shaky ground, my stalled H-1B visa, and my deteriorating financial situation, I was forced to consider the idea of returning to India for good. But I had told myself all along that if I ever returned, it would be of my own volition and a deliberate choice—just as coming to the United States had been.

AS THE SITUATION with Rebecca worsened, I receded further into our shared house, spending most of the time confined to my room and away from any of the common areas. One evening, as I read quietly in my room, I heard her voice rising in anger and the sound of cans being kicked around. I thought she was shouting again at her cat. But the next moment she was right outside my door.

"You just can't figure out how to recycle the correct way, can you?" she shouted at me.

"Is there a problem?" I asked.

"Is there a problem? Is there a bloody problem?" She was now in my room, just a few feet away from me.

"I know you're upset, but there's no reason to speak to me this way," I said.

She stood there seething for a minute, then turned abruptly and walked out of the room.

My heart beat very fast and my hands shook. Rebecca's verbal attack scared me more than I had ever been in my life. I thought of the long saws in the kitchen that she had lovingly sharpened just some days ago. I knew I had to leave. Not tomorrow, not at the end of the month when my lease ran out, but now. My hands continued to shake as I quickly packed a small tote bag. I didn't want my departure to be obvious, lest she stop me from leaving. I just wanted to make it to my car safely.

I looked around the room knowing that I would never be back, then stepped out into the living room. I walked past Rebecca with the tote bag on one shoulder. She was on the sofa watching TV, her cat on her lap, a vision of domestic bliss, as if nothing out of the ordinary had transpired just a few minutes ago. I held my breath as I walked to the door, but she didn't say a word.

It was 10:20 p.m. I got into my car and started driving south on I-880, past downtown Oakland, past Hayward and Fremont, not stopping until I reached Vikram's apartment an hour away in Santa Clara. He opened the door and was surprised to see me. I leaned against him and began to cry. In that moment, I was not sure what upset me more: that I had escaped a dangerous situation, or that I was once again seeking refuge under Vikram's roof.

15

The World Ends

My morning alarm went off as usual, set to KQED, the Bay Area's National Public Radio channel. But the news didn't sound the way it did on most other days: in the background to Bob Edwards' calm and measured voice was ominous music, a dirge almost, that would play for the next several days, a backdrop to the events of that day and all that followed. "One tower came down and then the other . . . New York City is paralyzed."

I flung off the covers and sprinted to the television in the living room and turned it on. It was only 6:15 a.m. in California, but it was 9:15 a.m. in New York. Two planes had struck the Twin Towers of the World Trade Center. It was September 11, one day after my thirty-first birthday.

On the television screen I watched the two planes smash their way into the towers over and over again, in slow motion, followed by the tall plumes of flames, roiling balls of white smoke, and the avalanche of ash bearing down on the streets as people ran helter-skelter. This was not an accident but a deliberate act of terrorism.

I changed quickly and went into the office. There was silence everywhere, but the sound of fear was palpable and loud—

a high decibel wail that no one could hear but all could feel. MPR's president called a meeting at eleven.

"You can all go home if you want. Go get your kids, do what you need to do to feel safe," he said.

We were all worried. One of the hijacked planes had been destined for San Francisco. Was it because those were the longest domestic flights, with planes carrying more fuel, capable of producing bigger explosions and maximum destruction? Or was the Bay Area a target of the terrorist attack, with perhaps more to come? No one knew. Meanwhile, there were three bridges in the Bay Area that were under surveillance, and many of my colleagues had to travel on those bridges to get back home.

In the days that followed, details began to emerge about the men who'd piloted the planes into the buildings. Their faces appeared on television screens across American living rooms, all of them Middle Eastern, most bearded, some turbaned. And one fact stood out: one of the men was in the US on an F-1 student visa to pursue training courses at a flight school. The same type of visa that had allowed me to enter and remain in the US, and on which thousands of international students enter the US each year from over two hundred countries.

Hani Hanjour, a Saudi Arabian, piloted the plane that was flown into the Pentagon. Hanjour had been admitted to a flight academy in California and then moved to a flight school in Arizona. But he struggled with the flight training and soon dropped out, returning to Saudi Arabia at the end of November 1996. He did not overstay his student visa, as was commonly believed. And he was the only one of the nineteen hijackers with a student visa, not one of several as falsely reported.

As the US reeled from the aftermath of 9/11, the impact of

the attack went far beyond the nearly three thousand who died that day. The American flag, once a simple symbol of American patriotism, now began to appear everywhere as an expression of solidarity. Nearly thirty-six thousand units of blood were donated to the New York Blood Center in the days after the September 11 attacks. It was possible to donate to the Red Cross with just one click on Amazon, and the organization raised $3 million in just two days.

It also became clear to me that modern Americans were dealing with the notion of terrorism more directly and viscerally than ever before. Many reported symptoms of stress and depression after the attacks. For the first time, there was a growing awareness that there were parts of the world that didn't share in the sunny optimism and unquestioned exuberance of America. In the most unexpected way, 9/11 forced Americans to expand their geography and the boundaries of their knowledge beyond the West. For the first time, there was an awareness of the "stans"—Pakistan, Afghanistan, Kazakhstan, Uzbekistan, Turkmenistan. Where once my graduate school classmates had questioned whether India was indeed in Asia, many Americans could now identify the ancient towns of Kandahar and Kabul. Five years after 9/11, the US Department of Defense launched a National Security Language Initiative designed to educate future generations of American school and college students in eleven languages that would help them understand little-known countries that might represent threats to the US. Colleges and universities began to offer programs in Middle East studies and Arabic language.

But where I came from, terrorism had long been a part of our daily reality. In India, there was no attempt to color-code the terrorist threat level or launch expensive scholarship programs to build mutual understanding. It was understood that the randomness of terrorist attacks made them so terrorizing in the first place—it all boiled down to sheer bad luck and being in the wrong place at the wrong time. In the 1980s India had witnessed a series of terrorist incidents, culminating in the gruesome attack on Rajiv Gandhi, India's cherubic, amiable prime minister—a yesteryear Justin Trudeau with an Italian wife to boot—in which a young Sri Lankan woman from a separatist group detonated herself as she bent down to touch his feet in a gesture of respect. After 9/11 came the terrorist attack on the Indian Parliament in December 2001, a bold move designed to destroy the epicenter of Indian political power. And then on November 26, 2008, seven years after 9/11, ten members suspected of belonging to *Lashkar-e-Taiba* (Army of the Righteous), an Islamic militant group based in Pakistan, carried out a series of twelve coordinated shooting and bombing attacks in Mumbai. In what became known as the 26/11 attacks, 174 people died and over three hundred were wounded as the terrorists held the city under siege for four days.

But there was something different about the 9/11 attacks on America. The sheer audacity and scale of the attacks stunned even the most cynical and battle weary. Never before had technology and aeronautical know-how been marshaled to cause such shock and awe. It was a cold and calculated act, and America's loss that day was also the world's loss. The dead that day included 372 citizens from over ninety countries, including forty-one Indians. Many of them had come to the US as international students and, like me, had been through the rigors of obtaining an H-1B visa. They were working at top global firms like Cantor

Fitzgerald, immersed in corporate America, when the planes struck.

The more I looked around me, the uncannier were the connections between the world that was torn down, between the US and India, and the world that emerged after 9/11. Anybody who looked South Asian or Middle Eastern and was male was a potential hate crime target, with nearly six hundred incidents reported in the first ten days after the attacks. Five hundred furious people mobbed a Chicago-area mosque and refused to leave until they were forced out by police. A Pakistani grocer was murdered in Texas. A Sikh gas station owner in Arizona was shot, his signature turban mistaken for the headwraps worn by Osama Bin Laden and his men.

As the suspicion toward outsiders grew, so did the twists and ironies. After the Twin Towers came down, a third building close by collapsed later in the day. The cause for the collapse of World Trade Center 7, as it was known, remained a mystery for many years as it was not hit by the two planes. The lead investigator was Shyam Sunder, once an international student from India, who'd arrived in the US in 1977 to pursue his graduate studies in engineering at MIT. I was struck by the irony of an engineer who had come to the US as a student now helping to solve the crime that another foreign student—Hani Hanjour, one of the 9/11 terrorists—had been accused of committing.

The connections between India and 9/11 did not end there. Just six months after the attacks, India imported seventy thousand tons of wreckage from the WTC site. While post-9/11 workers in New York tried to protect themselves from the toxic debris, industries in India saw an opportunity to repurpose the strong steel rods from the towers, flouting the warnings of

Greenpeace and other environmental groups about the health and environmental hazards. Today, at least three very different places in India—a college in Kerala, a car maintenance yard in Tamil Nadu, and a textile showroom in Punjab—have been built up from the steel scrap of the Twin Towers. Was it an inevitable cycle of destruction and rebirth, I wondered, in which the collapse of an American symbol of affluence and success could give rise to something like a college, a place of learning? Or was the reality more depressing: that anything American, however damaged and destroyed, was considered superior to its Indian counterpart?

MEANWHILE, MY OWN life was in turmoil. My H-1B visa had finally come through in May 2000 after a six-month wait. After fleeing from Rebecca's place that night, I was back to looking for a home, knowing that this time I would need to live on my own —no more roommates for me, ever.

I finally found an apartment in the city of Oakland, on the border of Berkeley, where my office was situated. Many of my Indian friends, ensconced comfortably in their suburban Silicon Valley subdivisions, tried their best to dissuade me, citing the high crime rate in Oakland and its large Black population. But driving around the city, I loved what I saw: the charming Victorian houses, the curving sweep of Lake Merritt with its historic structures and the necklace of lights, and the iconic Grand Lake Theatre. The gentrification along racial and economic lines, and the separation of "safe" and "dangerous" areas, seemed to be no different than in any other large city in the US, or even any different from some of India's large metros. I eventually picked an apartment close to Oakland's famous Piedmont Avenue, known for its cafés, restaurants, and boutiques.

The apartment building had a live-in property manager, Thelma, an elderly lady whose apartment was down the hall from mine. A sign on her front door read: I AM NOT A PACK RAT, I AM A COLLECTOR. Every inch of space in her apartment displayed the bric-a-brac she collected from the yard sales she attended on Saturday mornings. She bought anything that was of any conceivable use: small kitchen appliances, plant stands, a metal wine rack, a glass cake stand, small wooden stools. There were brightly colored artificial flowers and plants, potted with soil to create the illusion of being real. Then there were the painted wooden birdhouses, dozens of them, lining the tops of Thelma's kitchen cabinets. What could not be accommodated in her overflowing apartment was placed outside her front door with a "For Sale" sticker and was typically resold at a higher price, generating some extra income for her.

My apartment was a large one-bedroom. Now I would have to furnish it. While moving out of Vikram's place, I had chosen to leave behind all of its contents. It was going to be hard enough for me to figure out how to organize, digest, and shelve the memories of our ten years together; the last thing I wanted was to surround myself with things that reminded me of our planned future. And those things had been plentiful. Vikram and I had continued to fill our lives with shared objects even as our relationship was fast dissolving. It was as if we could fill the widening abyss between us with the Indian block-print curtains that we both liked, or the cedar chest that would store our woolens, that these objects would somehow block our exit from a foundering relationship. But all the issues between us eventually overwhelmed these futile efforts at forging a connection.

We separated our bank accounts, and I began to expunge all traces of our relationship from my closets, from my bookshelves, from the kitchen, and from all my important decisions—like a cold, methodical criminal cleaning up the scene of a crime. Over time, I began to fill my apartment with furniture that only I had picked out, that didn't need a second opinion. My first big purchase was a bright red couch, and I had already bought my first car, a deep blue Volks-wagen Jetta.

But I discovered that moving on was more difficult than I had anticipated. A deep, dull heaviness settled into my day each time I came across old writing pads with Vikram's doodles, or mathematical notations in his neat handwriting from the time he coached me through my statistics class. There were the books, many of them inscribed with affectionate messages from him.

During our days as struggling international students, between saving for a car and air tickets to India, we had also managed to buy each other small gifts over the years. There was the large Coca-Cola polar bear Vikram had bought me on a Valentine's Day when I was sick with the flu, and the two soft toys he had won as prizes at the State Fair in North Carolina for which we had saved money all week to afford the ten-dollar entry per person. But most of Vikram's gifts had been utilitarian: a sturdy microwave, a leather portfolio bag to replace a sporty backpack that I loathed but was the only bag I could afford, and a brand-new TV the first time we began to live separately during one of our many "taking-a-break-from-the-relationship," "together-but-apart" phases. Just like our relationship, these gifts were solid and reliable, adding a comforting predictability to my life. Or so I thought. Now, ten years later, I needed to distance myself from the detritus of what could have been but wasn't.

I was no longer an international student on an F-1 visa; I'd escaped the harsh immigration rules and widespread distrust of international students that immediately followed 9/11. I also felt a guilty relief at not being a Muslim, and in being a woman: being female somehow protected me from the worst of the suspicion that followed 9/11. But even so, it felt as if the world around me was crumbling. The dot-com bubble in Silicon Valley had also burst, crushing the entrepreneurial dreams of twentysomething techies, which included many of the Indian Americans I knew. It was the end of an era—for me, for international students, and for the US. It was a moment to pause, take stock, and reassess the path forward.

16

Code Switching:
Resident Alien and Nonresident Indian

I stood outside the carved iron gates of Indraprastha College, debating whether to go in and see the professors who had taught me many years ago. This is where my journey had begun almost fifteen years ago, when traveling to America had just been an idea. But nothing seemed to have changed: the same *chaat-walla* was outside the college gate with his cart, selling his special brand of tangy potato *chaat*, and groups of young women —some in their *salwar kameezes*, others in jeans—lingered at the gates. That was me, fifteen years earlier. Like many immigrants-in-the-making in America, Vikram and I had always told ourselves that it was merely a matter of time before we would return to India for good. Returning home had been our shared dream, not my dream to pursue alone. We planned to buy a cottage in a quaint hill station, our holiday escape, with Vikram paying 75 percent of the price and I would pay 25 percent. I never questioned the logic of the formula, but perhaps it was always assumed that he would earn more than I ever would.

But the right moment to return home never seemed to arrive. After six years in graduate school, it seemed rash to forgo the one year of US employment available to us through Optional Practical Training. Once that ended, it only made sense to take advantage of more work experience in America and the earnings that would help us make up for our frugal graduate school years. Then the dream of returning home became increasingly elusive as my relationship with Vikram ended and as each of us continued down the path of what defined success in America.

Now, thirteen years after coming to the US, I had acquired many of the trappings of the American dream: real estate in the San Francisco Bay Area, one of the most expensive parts of the country; 401K retirement savings; and all kinds of insurance— auto, health, dental, property, travel—that covered me from head to toe and then some. As for Vikram, he was even further entrenched in the US: he was now married to an Indian American who had been born and raised in Pennsylvania.

But my desire to return to India wouldn't go away. I decided to take the plunge. In June 2005, after a year of planning, I took a six-month leave of absence from my job in California, rented my apartment, canceled all my many insurance policies, and caught an Air India flight to New Delhi. It was a one-way ticket, the only one-way ticket I'd ever bought other than the one in 1992 to come to America. I was setting out on my own, exploring a return to India, and recalibrating my life and my dreams.

MY PLAN TO return to India was bolstered by the fact that I now possessed a coveted green card, the document that made me a "resident alien" in the US. The card gave me a safety net because it meant I could always return to the US if things didn't work out for me in India.

The green card was given its name not because it signifies a "green light" or permission to live in the US, but because the version issued after World War II was printed on pale green paper. The HR department at MPR had never filed for a green card for an employee. They offered to split the cost of the green card with me and to give me a loan for the amount that I would need to pay for my share. Their rationale was that, by applying for one, I was investing in my future and should cover part of the cost. This seemed fair to me. But MPR did not have an in-house legal counsel who could help prepare and submit my green card application, so they gave me the freedom to pick my own lawyer.

I approached Sheela Murthy, a well-known immigration lawyer based in Maryland. I had been reading her website for a few years now, and her name was mentioned on various listservs. I was nervous about the process, but having one of the best immigration lawyers in the country gave me some confidence. Sheela was originally from India and had set up her immigration practice in response to the long and tedious four-year process that she and her husband went through to obtain their green cards.

Most of my friends who were going from an H-1B to a green card were applying through the Employment-Based EB3 category which required "labor certification," a lengthy process in which their employer, once again, had to prove that there was no equally qualified American for the job. But a special preference category, called the EB1, existed for someone like me, who had obtained a PhD from a US college or university and was regarded as a high-priority worker. The EB1 provides permanent residency for foreign nationals who either have "extraordinary abilities" or are "outstanding professors or researchers" who "are recognized internationally for their outstanding academic achievements in a particular field."

To prove my value to the US, I had to obtain ten letters of recommendation from experts in my field who would help make the case that not letting me immigrate to the US would be a loss of US-trained talent for the country. It felt awkward and humbling, but I reminded myself that it could have been worse: I might have been subjected to the labor certification process and had my green card rejected if MPR was unable to prove that they couldn't find anyone else to fill my job.

The next step in the process was a medical exam by a civil surgeon. The US wanted not just the best talent but also the healthiest and strongest, eliminating those that were infirm—a modern-day version of the physical examinations that immigrants underwent at Ellis Island. The health form asked about every condition imaginable, from tuberculosis to sexually transmitted diseases. A "yes" to any of the questions would mean that my green card application was in trouble. The exam left me feeling dirty and tainted.

I was lucky to receive my green card in a year; many others around me had to wait far longer for their green cards to come through. Rohit Sareen had arrived in the US around the same time as me, also planning to study at a university in North Carolina. He and his employer encountered every hurdle imaginable in his efforts to obtain a green card. The problems included lawyers at a first job who didn't file for immigration paperwork on time and missed a deadline, resulting in Rohit's sudden inability to work; the occurrence of 9/11 and a two-year delay in processing because his application file was being shuttled between two agencies; and repeated lapses and renewals of his

H-1B visa. By the time Rohit received his green card, a full ten years had passed, and he had spent thousands of dollars on visa renewals and application fees. But there are stories worse than his and he still considers himself one of the lucky few as he had no dependents and had a very supportive employer.

FEELING SECURE WITH my newly acquired green card, I made plans to move back to India in 2005 which, by all accounts, would be a bumper year for Indians returning home. The Indian economy was booming and jobs were plentiful. The bursting of the Silicon Valley bubble in 2002 had forced many Indians to abandon their Californian dreams and return to India, while others had returned following the wave of animosity toward South Asians and all brown people following 9/11.

It seemed like an opportune time for me to join the flow of those headed home. In the year leading up to my departure for India, I applied for at least twelve jobs in India. But there was no response, not even a polite acknowledgment of my email or query. Other friends who had recently relocated to India insisted that there was no way that I could accomplish my goal long-distance, and that I would simply have to take time off from my life in the US and plant myself in India for a period of time.

Upon arriving in India and ready to apply for jobs, I set myself up for three weeks in Delhi to network and meet with people. Delhi is to India what Washington, DC, is to the US—the hub of government, nonprofit, and international activity. When I had left India thirteen years ago, I had been a student and had never been exposed to the culture of work. I now had a lot to learn about how the Indian workplace functioned. To begin with, I discovered that people in India often didn't return calls and didn't like to make appointments too far in advance.

"Why don't you stop by any day after eleven a.m.?" was the vague kind of response that I often received, with 11:00 a.m. seeming to be a magic hour for meetings and optimal productivity—late enough to allow for a leisurely start to the day, and early enough not to cut into the lunch hour.

Another problem I encountered was the Indian obsession with personal connections. I thought back to the words of the man sitting next to me on the flight back to India who said: "Until the day India becomes about *what* you know rather than *who* you know, it will not progress." I soon discovered that he was right. I had to use all my connections and pull every string I could think of just to line up interviews. When I did approach employers without some kind of reference or introduction, I was treated with utter rudeness at worst and complete indifference at best. Even getting beyond the security guards at organizations like the Population Council, UNICEF, and UNESCO was impossible. Moreover, having a foreign credential from the US didn't automatically open doors as I had expected. India now had plenty of people with degrees from top institutions in the UK, the US, and Australia.

My social science background posed yet another difficulty. The booming sectors of IT and finance had benefited the most from the recent flow of returnees from abroad, leaving little room for social scientists, teachers, and people like me. The bias in favor of science and engineering that had dogged me when I was a college student in Delhi was still evident in the job market. Many social sector organizations were staffed not by experts in development, population, the environment, or education, but rather by retired bureaucrats who—apart from their general administrative and planning skills—had little to contribute by way of sector-specific substance and knowledge. India's political scientists, applied psychologists, sociologists, economists, and policy analysts seemed to have few employment opportunities outside universities, and even fewer options that were lucrative and had growth potential.

I explored jobs in India's burgeoning Non-Governmental Organization (NGO) sector as well. Most grassroots Indian NGOs continued to be underfunded, but some were doing extremely well, with plenty of foreign funding from international aid agencies such as the UN, the UK's Department for International Development (DFID), and others. The senior staff at these organizations were a tight-knit clique. Many were foreign-educated and spouted global development-speak, yet adhered to a carefully cultivated earthy, intellectual image. Dressed in homespun FabIndia kurtas, they toted the latest personal gadgets and hobnobbed with other intelligentsia at Delhi hotspots such as the Habitat Centre and the India International Centre. But in these circles, too, the employment opportunities seemed to be scarce, and I didn't have the required connections.

Perhaps most daunting of all, I wasn't just a foreign-returned graduate seeking a job, but was a woman seeking a professional fit in a male-dominated workplace. At every meeting with senior officials, most of whom were male, I was expected to display a deferential and subservient attitude, referring to them as "sir" and kowtowing to an antiquated dynamic to which I was no longer accustomed. I thought about my male professors at NC State, who had encouraged me to call them by their first names. What I had dismissed then as the casualness of Am culture, I now realized was also an attempt to break down the power structures between men and women that have long existed in every setting, from the classroom to the office. During my time in the US, I had become used to being treated as an equal, speaking to men as equals.

But here in India, everywhere I looked, whether it was supposedly new and progressive higher education institutes or cutting-edge private sector companies, all appeared to be male bastions of power where women scurried around responding to the orders of men in high positions. At a management institute where I interviewed for a job, of the thirty-six full-time faculty, only four were women and only one was a full professor. I boarded flights that were filled mostly with men; a business lunch of executives from Reliance, one of India's largest companies, included all men; and women were often missing altogether from conference panels and from meetings.

Of course, some of these issues existed in the US too, whether it was the low representation of women in C-suites and leadership roles, the disparity in pay that I had experienced at one of my first jobs at the youth program in Raleigh, the prevalence of sexual assault and oppression, or the intersecting issues of skin color and gender that pushed Black or brown American women to lighten their skin—just like their Indian counterparts—to mirror a global ideal of Caucasian beauty. When it came to these global issues, I concluded that India sat toward one end of the spectrum while the US was closer to the other end—not perfect, by any means, but offering women like me better options.

The more I thought about my place in a male-dominated work environment in India, I realized that there were practical issues to consider, too, and that I simply could not live on the salaries I was being offered. As someone who worked on the "softer" side of science and research and in a field not known for its earning power, I had long ago resigned myself to a life of modest comforts. But even by Indian standards, the salaries I was offered couldn't sustain an urban lifestyle in an expensive city like Delhi.

The city had transformed itself into a stylish metropolis in the years I had been away. Every exotic ingredient imaginable was now available to satisfy the discerning tastes of globe-trotting Indian gourmands, designer denims had replaced elegant saris at evening shindigs, and wine bars and Italian coffee shops dotted the city. Those who could afford these indulgences were either the up-and-coming Indian nouveau riche or foreign-returned Indians in high tech and finance, many with salaries in dollars that enabled them to replicate the lives they once enjoyed abroad. Their children went to international schools to be educated in an all-American curriculum, and they transported themselves and their families from place to place in imported air-conditioned cars that sealed out the pollution and poverty, inconvenient reminders that they were, in fact, living in a developing country.

All the times I had thought about returning, I had imagined living in the real India, not an insulated bubble of Western and first-world comforts. But I no longer knew what the real India was, and it was perhaps I who was the misfit, trapped in an India of my imagination that was long gone.

AFTER THREE WEEKS of job hunting in Delhi and little luck, I went home to Bhopal to be with my mother. Both she and my father seemed neutral about my efforts to return to India. My father, always the pragmatist, wanted me to live wherever the best opportunities were and, in his assessment, there could be no better place for that than the US. My mother missed me terribly when I lived in the US, but her visits there had shown her the freedoms and first-world living I enjoyed there, which she knew would never be available to me in India.

Back in Bhopal, I went to the same sort of inane parties I had attended on each visit home. It was the same people, with a bit more gray hair and more money. But this time there was a difference: nobody asked me anymore when I was getting married. I was relieved because it meant that I didn't have to talk about Vikram, the mysterious fiancé they had heard about all these years but never met. But it was also a tacit reminder that, in the eyes of most Indians, I had now officially entered spinsterhood. Once past thirty, one was written off as no longer desirable and certainly not eligible.

And something else had also changed, not in them but in me. I found myself defending America and Americans in a way that I never had before. Where earlier I might have joined in the criticism of all things American, I now bristled at the generalizations that were bandied about so casually at such parties.

"There are no family values in America!" "The children have no respect for elders!"

"Everyone is just so free with each other!" In response to this, I argued that many Indian families hid sordid stories of sexual abuse of young girls at the hands of their male relatives. What of that?

"America is just such a materialistic society!" This dismissal of American society was offered as the Bhopal jet set sat around drinking Scotch and eating imported cheese while their house help could barely afford to buy milk.

The truth was that I too was constantly comparing America and India, weighing the merits of one against the other, especially as I tried to make the weighty decision of where to work and live. One was arguably the world's most advanced and developed country; the other, still a developing country, albeit one of the world's fastest growing economies. There was much optimism and chest-thumping about India being the fastest growing high-tech capital of the world, and a magnet for business and private sector entrepreneurship. To showcase the ambitions of a bold and global India, the Indian government launched slick marketing campaigns with themes like *India Shining* and *Incredible India*.

But despite all this progress, India still seemed to be lagging significantly when it came to basics such as civic conveniences and health care, faring worse in key statistics than even Bangladesh, Sri Lanka, Bhutan, Sudan, and Equatorial Guinea. The irony didn't escape me that, while India had just one doctor for every 1,457 people, well below the World Health Organization's recommendation, the country provided the largest number of international medical graduates to the US and was the world's largest supplier of immigrant physicians.

The Indians I spoke with about these matters didn't appreciate my observations. Now that I was a "Nonresident Indian" (NRI), it appeared that I had lost the right to voice any complaints about India. Whether I protested meekly about the health care system, nonfunctional taxi meters, or corrupt politicians—all things that Indians themselves complained about bitterly day in and day out—I was promptly admonished, "This is not your America," as if to say that Indians themselves couldn't be expected to have high expectations of their government or their standard of living. In India I was too American, and in America I was too Indian. An outsider in both places.

Wherever I went in India and especially at job interviews, I encountered a certain bafflement at my decision: having gone through the tortuous immigration process in the US, why on earth would I consider giving all of that up to return to India? After all, newspapers regularly cited market surveys of Indian students that revealed that, all things being equal, the average Indian student wanted to leave India to study in the US. These people were supposed to be recruiting me for a job, yet here they were, wondering why I even wanted to move back to India in the first place. One woman, a professor at a management school in Delhi who'd experienced a one-year stint in London with her family, told me that, given the choice, she would never have returned to India. But her husband had insisted on returning, and so she followed.

Why did I want to return to India? Why, indeed? I didn't have a traditional conservative family that insisted I return, and nor was I the scion to a family empire and inheritance that awaited my return. I barely had any friends left in India. Like me, they had all left and settled abroad, whether in the US, Singapore, the UK, Hong Kong, or Australia. And I was not following a partner or spouse who needed to relocate.

My desire to return to India came down to a sense of idealism, perhaps misplaced. I didn't want to become "one of those"—the millions who had left India and now remained trapped in first-world honey. I thought I was better than all of them, that I would return to give back to India in some small measure what it had given me.

"India needs you," said a patriotic family friend, hoping to convince me to return. But after six months of trying to find my place in India, I was no longer sure this was true.

All those who questioned my desire to return to India didn't understand what it felt like to be an immigrant, strung between two worlds, a constantly fragmented existence. One foot here and one foot there, juggling two time zones, two systems of measurement, and two cultures. I was tired of the never-ending dance. Those who had never left home could not understand the homesickness that often caught me unawares, washing over me in waves, as I thought about the first drops of rain on dry earth that heralded the Indian monsoon, or as I longed to eat an Indian mango whose sweetness reminded me of carefree childhood summers spent feasting on buckets of chilled mangoes. They could not understand the almost visceral longing to return.

After six months in India, I had made my decision. That night in Delhi, the city where I was born and the foundation for the first twenty-one years of my life in India, I went up to the roof of my grandparents' house. The sky was a dull gray-pink, the colors of dusk muted by the ever-present smog. Flocks of parakeets roosted in nearby trees. Clusters of houses stretched out in the horizon, mingling with the dilapidated domes and soaring minarets of Delhi's ancient Mughal monuments. As the sky darkened, lights began to twinkle. This is how I would always remember Delhi.

Could I ever return to live here? The answer was no; there was nothing more for me here. India and I had both changed and grown, but in different directions. I had become a foreigner in my own country.

17

A New Beginning

Once I let go of the dream of returning to India, I felt liberated. For the first time in many months, I allowed myself to relax. I planned a trip to Goa, the prime resort destination in India, to unwind and soak in some sun and sand. There, on Goa's famed beaches and amidst its historic Portuguese mansions and unusual Hindu temples, I contemplated my next steps.

The door to my future opened one day at a small internet café in Panjim, Goa's capital city, where I had gone to check my email and scan job sites. The Institute of International Education (IIE) in New York was looking for a director of research and evaluation. The job had everything I was looking for. It was international in nature. After being turned away from UN- and World Bank-type jobs for so many years, I still harbored the desire to do more international work. Now the opportunity had presented itself. IIE was one of the oldest and most venerable nonprofits in the US in the field of international education and exchanges. It was famous for having launched the Fulbright program for the US government in the 1950s, and for persuading Congress to create the F-1 international student visa in 1921. The only catch was that I had missed the application date by a couple of days. But I applied for the job anyway.

It felt surreal to apply for a job in New York City from an internet café thousands of miles away in Goa. But IIE responded quickly with an expression of interest. The organization needed to fill the position right away, and the only way for me to interview with them was over video conference. Skype had been around for a few years, but its bandwidth was typically slow, hardly suitable for a professional interview. I returned to Bhopal and arranged to rent space at a Reliance World Center that offered state-of-the art videoconferencing facilities, while IIE agreed to cover the high cost—Rs. 5,500 for thirty minutes, which was a lot less than what they might have spent on flying a candidate out to New York for an interview. During the interview, I looked like a professional newscaster, facing the camera from a wraparound desk with a large map of the world as the backdrop.

I got the job. It was a leap of faith for IIE and for me: they had never met me in person, and I had agreed to take a job in New York without having visited the office or meeting anyone who worked there. But it felt right. "Do you already have a green card?" they had asked, and for once I could say "yes" and simply move on. My immigration status in the US no longer felt like a weight that dragged me down or the lens through which my future employer would view me. There was no lowballing of the job offer, no desperation at my end. I could finally accept a new job on my own terms. I was more than my immigration status.

SIX MONTHS EARLIER, I had set out on a personal quest to move back to India. Now, I was moving from California to New York, which was geographically and culturally at the opposite end of the continent. Yet this move was nothing like the one I had made from North Carolina to California years before. I was leaving California on my own terms, leaving behind my relationship with Vikram and all the associations it carried. For the first time in my adult life, I was moving for myself and not because I was following someone, as I had done throughout my twenties.

I flew back to California in December 2005. I had just three weeks to wrap up my six years there: putting my condo on the market, sorting through my paperwork at the office, holding a moving sale, selling my car, and lining up the movers that my new company was willing to cover. I couldn't bring myself to throw away the soft toys I had hidden away in my closet, so I gave them to my best friend's little son. I took my engagement ring to an Indian jeweler in Fremont and asked him to exchange it for something else.

"Are you sure?" he said. "I can just as easily melt it and make something else out of it."

"No," I said. I didn't want to fashion the old into new; I wanted something completely different. I wanted my transition to New York City to be a new beginning in every sense of the term.

What I did not destroy were all the photographs of our years together. Even after our relationship ended, Vikram and I each had something the other didn't. Our early relationship in India had evolved through long letters written to each other in the times that we were apart, first within India in different cities, and then across thousands of miles when Vikram had just arrived in the US and I was still in India. He had with him the hundreds of letters we had written to each other, and I had all the photographs we had ever taken. I was the self-appointed photographer, the one always behind the camera, clicking photos with our friends and family.

We never thought then to make two copies. After we went our separate ways, Vikram asked me for the photos, but I never could find the time or perhaps the emotional resilience to sort through the hundreds of photos and negatives—not mere objects to be dispensed with, like the soft toys and books, but mileposts in a relationship that had spanned a decade.

By the time moving day arrived, I had purged, destroyed, or given away everything that I didn't need or couldn't sell. The movers arrived early, a team of four men, and took over the apartment. After all the years of hauling things myself during repeated moves, renting trucks and U-Hauls, I didn't have to do a thing this time around. I stood by and watched them wrap and pack each spoon and knife with speed and precision. But as I looked around to take inventory of the items, I saw that there was one thing that remained. It was a bedside reading lamp of brushed steel and glass that Vikram had bought for me in North Carolina. I wondered whether to take the lamp to New York. It was a lovely piece and a perfectly functional lamp. Still of two minds, I stuck a bright orange "Fragile" sticker on it and left the bedroom so the movers could proceed with the packing.

A few minutes later, I heard glass breaking and then a curse from my bedroom. I walked over to see what had happened. There lay the milky white glass lampshade of the reading lamp, shattered after seven years of careful use.

The man handling the lamp apologized. "I'm really sorry, ma'am. I'll file a claim," he said.

To his surprise, I smiled and shrugged. "It's fine, it doesn't matter," I said. "I hadn't really planned on taking the lamp with me, anyway."

I was moving on. It was a new beginning.

PART III

I remembered that the real world was wide, and that a varied field of hopes and fears, of sensations and excitements, awaited those who had the courage to go forth into its expanse, to seek real knowledge of life amidst its perils.

—CHARLOTTE BRONTË,
Jane Eyre

18

Made in America:
The Lure of a US Degree

I had arrived in New York City, the storied backdrop to almost every film about the US that I had seen before discovering the real America. After my ten-year failed relationship and a few unsuccessful efforts at dating, I had planned my move to NYC with great anticipation, imagining myself a Carrie Bradshaw from *Sex in the City*, stepping out of yellow cabs, looking up at the iconic Chrysler Building. Now, on the way to my new job, I passed the same building every morning, a silvery Art Deco beacon standing tall amidst the hubbub of the city below, and those very same yellow cabs whizzed around me. I went shopping for clothes at Century 21, the landmark store for marked-down designer wear and knockoffs. Working in Berkeley all those years, I had become accustomed to a casual workplace where people showed up in jeans and sweatshirts, but I'd heard that NYC was different, where everyone looked chic and strutted around in black. I bought wool pants and sweaters, and a business suit or two.

The Institute of International Education (IIE) was located across the street from the United Nations headquarters, where the row of country flags outside the UN fluttered majestically in the breeze. Was it sheer coincidence, I wondered, or the invisible hand of fate that had guided me here? It was my father's hope that I would someday work at the UN, which to him symbolized all that was global and elite. As I looked out over those flags, past the tall tower of the UN to the East River beyond, I realized that I had not only fulfilled his dream of studying in America, but that my office now overlooked the UN headquarters. There was no place on Earth that was more global, and I was now at the center of it.

My new job brought my fourteen years in the US full circle. I was to lead the work of researching and compiling the *Open Doors Report on International Educational Exchange*, an annually updated and widely used survey of thousands of US colleges and universities that, since the 1950s, had documented the number of international students and scholars coming to the US and the number of American students going abroad. It was a living record of the world's best minds and talent that had flowed into America and its universities over several decades, forever altering the landscape of American higher education and its relationship to the rest of the world.

On that sunny day in August 1992, when I had arrived in Raleigh as a fresh-faced and naive international student, I never imagined that I would one day lead the project in whose statistics I had appeared. My own journey to the US was now part of a phenomenon that I would study with the precision of a scientist—no longer an insider, but an outsider looking in.

I sat at my new desk and opened a copy of the 1992 edition of the *Open Doors Report*. It was a documentation of my own presence in the US, its blue cover faded and creased with frequent use. I turned the pages carefully. There I was, almost fourteen years ago: one among the thirty-six thousand students from India that year and 439,000 from around the world. Most Indian students that year were studying engineering, a larger number than any other group of international students in the US. In these numbers, I saw the faces of my international student friends—Ashish, Ravi, Gaurav—who'd filled the engineering department at NC State.

Today the number of international students in the US has grown to 1.1 million. All the years I had struggled—in the classroom, trying to make ends meet, and trying to find a job—I had imagined that my struggles were mine and mine alone. Now I was learning that they were the experiences and stories of millions of other international students, with their own shades and nuances, but united in the aspirations that had brought us here.

AS I BEGAN to learn more about the story of international students in the US, I wondered who had been the first intrepid student to cross borders to learn the American way. I found the answer much closer to home than I had expected.

In Cedar Hill Cemetery, just outside Hartford, Connecticut, and ninety-five miles from where I live, lies the unassuming grave of Yung Wing, who in 1854 became the first documented foreign student to graduate from a US university. I visited the cemetery on a crisp fall day as the hues from the changing colors bathed the historic cemetery in a golden light. The inscription on the elegant tombstone where Yung Wing's wife, Mary Kellogg, and he laid buried was in English, but in front of it was another stone with Chinese lettering. The two languages were a testament to the bridges that Yung Wing had attempted to build between the US and China.

Yung Wing arrived at Yale University on a scholarship arranged by Samuel Robbins Brown, an American missionary to China and Japan. After earning his degree, he was so inspired by his own experience that he went back to China's Qing Court to seek approval to bring more Chinese students to the US. The result was the Chinese Educational Mission, the first educational exchange between the US and China that brought 120 teenaged students over a decade to elite institutions like Yale, MIT, Harvard, and Columbia.

For this early group of Chinese students, it was a time of hope and excitement, buoyed by the potential of an American education and surrounded by the greatest inventions of the nineteenth century—the railroad, the telegraph, Alexander Graham Bell's telephone, and Thomas Edison's phonograph. But authorities in China became nervous over the growing American influence on their students. The Qing Court recalled the students to China. The students found an unlikely champion in the great American writer Mark Twain, who urged President Ulysses Grant to intervene to sustain the program. Yung Wing had lit the flame of desire in the minds of Chinese students to seek an American education. Today, 372,500 of them study in the US, the largest and most visible group of international students on American campuses.

But where did the Indian story begin? I wondered. By the time I had arrived in 1992, thirty-six thousand Indian students were already studying in the US, and these numbers have grown exponentially over the past thirty years, despite the barriers created by 9/11, periodic financial crises, and, most recently, the restrictive policies of the Trump administration.

Women's Medical College?
1886

???

The story of the long love affair between Indian students and US universities, it turns out, begins in the late 1800s. Long before me, and long before my uncle Satish who had arrived at Carnegie Mellon in the 1970s. Anandibai Joshee, a plucky young medical student, became the first Indian student to graduate in 1886 from a US institution—the Women's Medical College of Pennsylvania (now part of Drexel University). She went on to become the first Indian woman to be qualified as a physician. As with Yung Wing, I found that the connection to Anandibai was much closer to home than I could have imagined. Even though she had sailed back to India with the hope of beginning her work as a doctor, she fell ill and died at the age of twenty-two. To honor his wife's deep affection for America, Anandibai's husband sent her ashes to be buried in the US. Her final resting place is in Poughkeepsie Rural Cemetery in the Hudson Valley, an hour and a half from where I live. Far less grand than Yung Wing's headstone, her epitaph nonetheless reads: First Brahman woman to leave India to obtain an education.

For most Indians, England was still the preferred educational destination in the early 1900s, especially for those like my grandfather who planned to study law and appear for the Indian Civil Services exam. But a small number of Indian students began to look beyond England to the US, drawn to its reputation as the land of innovation, opportunity, and avant-garde ideas. There were just one hundred Indian students in the US in the early 1900s—or "Hindoos" as they were called, a name chosen not so much for religious reasons as from a need to differentiate them from Native American Indians. Indians were such a rare sight in the US that a telegram sent by Rathindranath Tagore— son of the Nobel Laureate poet Rabindranath Tagore—and a friend to the University of Illinois informing them of their arrival by train had been incorrectly transcribed as "Two students from Indiana."

Tagore became active in student services for foreign students at the University of Illinois, where he founded the first Cosmopolitan Club. By 1912, twelve such clubs had opened across the country, forming an important support system for international students. These clubs were the prototype for today's International Student Associations, which serve as a lifeline for students on US campuses. As a volunteer for the association on my campus, I lost count of the number of times I woke up early to drive to the Raleigh-Durham airport to pick up a bedraggled student who had just ended a twenty-four-hour journey. On other occasions, I would drive a group of new international students to the grocery store or demonstrate how the washing machines worked at the laundromat.

Indian students began making their voices heard on American campuses. Their growing involvement in US social and political movements soon led to the establishment of *The Hindusthanee Student: A quarterly review of education*, published by the Hindusthan Association of America (HAA), whose mission was to "further the interests of Hindustani students, and to interpret India to America and America to India." In a 1915 issue of the journal and in a paper titled *Why Should Hindu Girls Go to America*, a Miss. K. Tullaskar, who had received an MA from the University of Chicago, argued that all young Indian women needed to study in the US. She wrote the paper exactly eighty years before I acquired my master's degree from an American university, but her hopes and aspirations were the same as mine: the broadening of the mind through travel and education, and the fluidity of the American education system, which encouraged flexibility and experimentation as opposed to the memorization of rigid doctrines.

Almost fifty years later, K.D. Verma, an educator in Punjab, India, left home in 1963 to study at the University of Northern Iowa on a Ford Foundation scholarship. He landed in New York City with fourteen dollars in his pocket and bought a bus ticket to Iowa. Many years later, his son, Richard Verma, would become the twenty-fifth US ambassador to India under President Obama, the first Indian American to hold the position. The Verma family's story is one of seeking the best educational opportunities, wherever the search might lead. "Education has been the most important currency in my family for decades . . . education is the reason my father came to the US," Ambassador Verma shared with me.

BY 1913, 4,222 international students from around the world were enrolled in 275 US universities, colleges, and technical schools, most of them sent by foreign governments for education and training that would be useful when the students returned home.

Then came World War I. As the world convulsed and boundaries were drawn and redrawn, international students—particularly Europeans—were innocent victims of a new system of travel restrictions. Where education had once been insulated from political interests and knowledge had flowed freely across borders, international students and scholars were suddenly barred from coming to the US. In response, the IIE, where I was now working, was founded at the end of World War I by three

Nobel Peace Prize laureates. Its mission was to keep America's doors open to students and scholars from around the world at a time when the US was turning inwards and risked becoming isolated. IIE's President Stephen Duggan urged the US government to create a new type of visa for students, the F-1 visa, that would allow shiploads of European students to come to the US where they would remain in IIE's "custody." Waiting in a long line for my F-1 visa all those years ago, I could never have imagined that one day I would work for the very organization that had helped create the visa that would reopen the doors to international students in the US and on which millions of students still come to the US.

Now, as a researcher studying these trends, it was my job to understand, document, and report on the goals, challenges, and problems shared by international students from around the world. The work involved much more than compiling statistical data. I sought out international students from different countries, undergraduate and graduate, male and female, to understand what had brought them here, what kept some of them here, and what drove some of them to return home or to explore yet another destination. I began to realize that who comes to America to study and when is as much a personal choice and destiny as it is a mirror of world events, from the oil boom of the 1970s that allowed Middle Eastern countries flush with resources to send thousands of their students abroad, to the financial crises of the 1990s and 2008, to the loosening and tightening of immigration policies after 9/11 and under the Trump administration.

But history also repeats itself. In 2011, almost a hundred years after the US had become a haven for European scholars following World War I, US colleges and universities were once again trying to accommodate refugee students, this time from the war raging in Syria.

Sinan Zeino was one such student who shared his story with me. Back home at Al-Baath University in Syria, Sinan was pursuing an undergraduate degree in English Literature in 2013. As the war in Syria escalated, his days and nights were filled by the sounds of conflict—the airstrikes and artillery. Then one day, on his way to university, the bus in front of him exploded, killing everyone on board. Sinan knew he had to leave. After applying to several countries, he arrived at Salve Regina University in the US, a small, Catholic liberal arts institution in Rhode Island. He was the university's first scholarship student from war-ravaged Syria, but was one of many Syrian students who arrived at other US campuses, fleeing to survive and seeking a sense of safety and the ability to live freely.

But the sense of hope that Sinan and other refugee students like him have nurtured has slowly worn off as he continues to struggle with the complex, frustrating web of America's immigration system, unable to go home to Syria yet unable to feel rooted in his adoptive country—always on edge, always nervous, and always fleeing. The psychological toll of displacement that never went away, as I well knew from my grandmother's experience when she became a refugee, fleeing Pakistan for India.

I WANTED TO understand the global attraction of American colleges and universities. What is it about America that has drawn so many students since the nineteenth century? Why was an American education seen as the gold standard? Why had families like mine, all over Asia and other parts of the world, urged their children to look westwards even at the cost of separation and long distances, or even, most recently, at the risk of falling prey to the global pandemic caused by COVID-19?

For many students and their families, the answers to these questions seem obvious. Wisdom Omuya, a Nigerian who had come to the US as an international student in 2011, told me that most Nigerian families expected that their children would go abroad. And what was the perceived value of a US education? Wisdom responded that it was considered a matter of pride; it was like proving that you could "climb a mountain . . . a concrete way of demonstrating your ability to go toe to toe with the world." Later, at the height of the Coronavirus pandemic, I asked Suraj, a twelfth grader in India, why he wanted to go abroad. He, too, was puzzled by my question: in his family, it had always been assumed that he would go to the US. Wisdom and Suraj speak for millions of others around the globe.

But through my research I also learned that not all international students are the same. As I immersed myself in the *Open Doors* project and other surveys in the field, the data pointed to key differences. And I gained firsthand knowledge about these differences when I taught a class at Teachers College, Columbia University, on the topic of student mobility. We examined questions like: Why do students move around the world for an education? What motivates them? What does this migration look like?

Perhaps not by design but more as an artifact of the large presence of international students in most graduate schools across the US, half the students in the class were from other countries and the other half were Americans. For a social scientist like me, it was a living experiment in the very topic I was to teach.

Our classroom discussions revealed that some students— particularly from Europe—come to the US looking for the cul- tural exchange experience, following in the footsteps of generations of scholars from the West and even Yung Wing from the East, for whom crossing borders is a way of expanding the mind and learning about other countries and cultures. This is also the main motivation of American students who go abroad. Yet others, like students from India and China, are focused on the idea of America as a land of opportunity; they come to further their educational and professional trajectories, often going from student to permanent resident to even citizen, much as I had done. But even those who are focused on opportunity and a "return on investment" end up being transformed—an important by-product of their experience that they would only recognize much later. This was the case for me. I did not intentionally come to America seeking cultural exposure or some of the "softer" outcomes of an international experience, yet my fundamental values and beliefs—and even my sense of self and as a woman—were deeply shaped by my experience of being a student in America.

And then there is the notion of quality—an unequivocal hallmark of an American college or university. Survey after survey shows that millions of students around the world consistently rank the US as offering them the best quality education. To some, this quality is measured by how well American institutions do in the ever-competitive global rankings of institutions. For others from more conservative societies or countries with a rigid academic system, being on an American campus represents freedom, unfettered learning, and the flexibility to follow their interests. For many—particularly all the science and engineering students—it means access to the best professors, scientists, and research labs in the world, features that have made America the world leader in science and innovation.

But behind all these reasons is the quintessential and indefinable quality of America that has drawn seekers and students—a land of freedom, opportunity, and possibilities. A country that gave the world the Wild West, *Star Trek*, and *Indiana Jones*, where pushing boundaries and exploring new frontiers—real, psychological, and educational—seem possible. This is the essence of America, reflected in its colleges and universities, that has drawn students from all over the world, pioneers in their quest for knowledge and a better future.

International students, then, come to America for many reasons. They come for the education; they come for the American dream; they come because they have been pushed out of their home countries; they come because their countries sent them. That day when I stood at the consulate in Delhi, holding my breath before the officer who examined my papers, I hadn't realized I was following in the steps of others who had stood in similar lines and with similar anxieties at Ellis Island. So much had changed in the world since those days a century before, but one thing had remained the same: the enduring appeal of a made-in-America education.

19

Unofficial Ambassadors

Even though I was now an observer, an outsider researching the role that education was playing in America's relationship with the world, I often thought of the ways that America had influenced me, stealthily entering my consciousness and shaping my worldview. Music was one such way. I had grown up listening to Simon and Garfunkel, Michael Jackson, and Madonna, often unable to fully decipher their American accents and never understanding the context or motivations for their lyrics. It was a music that was quintessentially American in its experimentation and audacity, in its messages of self-discovery and independence.

Soon after coming to the US, I discovered jazz, quite by accident, as I tuned a radio one evening. Though the sounds of jazz were foreign to me, I began to notice a nonverbal conversation between the musicians, a playful competition that felt strangely familiar. The more I thought about it, the more I realized that it reminded me of Indian classical music, in which the ragas—similar to the standards in American jazz—remain the same, but are interpreted and performed differently by different artists. And the repartee between jazz musicians was like the *Jugalbandi* of Indian classical music, in which one musician plays a series of notes and cycles and challenges the other musician to follow suit, the spontaneous back-and-forth culminating in a crescendo where all the musicians come together again, playing in harmony.

Curious about this unexpected relationship between two completely different forms of music—one that originated among the slaves on American plantations and the other in the Vedic hymns of Indian temples—I began to discover that the music of jazz greats such as John Coltrane and Miles Davis had been influenced by Indian classical music. And, conversely, the popularity of jazz in India in the 1950s wasn't accidental but was a deliberate strategy on the part of the US government to spread goodwill across the world through something as benign yet influential like music. American popular music became a powerful form of soft diplomacy. "America's secret weapon is a blue note in a minor key," quipped the *New York Times* in 1955 when Louis Armstrong toured the world.

Religion played a role in America's soft diplomacy as well. Before any educational or cultural exchanges or any structured, formal efforts by the US government to engage with the world, there was the pervasive spread of Christianity and efforts to spread the gospel far and wide. I discovered to my surprise that the *Open Doors* survey had once been called *Unofficial Ambassadors* and that its origins lay in a 1925 survey by the Committee on Friendly Relations Among Foreign Students, a collection of American Christian organizations formed to welcome foreign students with the hope of introducing them to Christianity. The survey found that most students who declared themselves to be Christians were from non-Western places like the Philippines, Korea, and Latin America, regions where Christianity had a long and complex history, as well as from China, Japan, and India. If these students stayed on in the US, they were likely to become future converts, like Steve whom I had met as a graduate student on that balmy evening in North Carolina and who had proudly embraced Christianity and rejected Hinduism. And if they went back home, they would help take Christianity back to their communities and societies, helping spread the religion far and wide. Religion also seemed to provide a crutch for international students during difficult times, when they were the most vulnerable and needy.

American efforts to proselytize and spread Christianity soon morphed into a tool for US diplomacy, a mix of philanthropy and politics that continued to evolve to suit America's national goals and priorities. For most of the twentieth century, international students like me had been an unexamined entity whose presence on US campuses was unobtrusive yet helped inject a dose of internationalism that spoke to the altruism of America. The mutual exchange of ideas and learning was generally thought of as a good thing, supported across the US political spectrum and rarely questioned.

This type of soft power was a cornerstone of American diplomacy as early as the First World War. It crested in the late-1940s with the launch of the Fulbright scholarship program, America's flagship exchange initiative. The program had been proposed in 1945, when Senator J. William Fulbright suggested that the debt that other countries owed the US for war-related equipment and supplies be redirected into educational and cultural exchange programs, as if to quite literally channel "swords into plowshares of the mind." Under the auspices of IIE, the Fulbright program would eventually bring scholars from all over the world to study in the US while sending Americans overseas. To this day, it remains the most prestigious and influential scholarship program in history and a "megaphone to transmit American ideas to the world."

That megaphone was indeed effective. By the time I was growing up in India, the word Fulbright had become almost a household term, evoking prestige and accomplishment—the greatest honor bestowed on scholars and intellectuals. India has one of the largest Fulbright programs and twenty thousand Indians and Americans have received Fulbrights to study in each other's country. Yet it maintains its mystique as a privilege available to a select few. My mother, a professor in the small city of Bhopal, applied for a Fulbright several times, but it remained a shiny object always out of her reach, seemingly reserved for those from India's most elite universities. And here I was now, working for the organization that had designed and launched the program and still runs it today.

The scope and reach of the Fulbright Program today is unparalleled. Operating in over 160 countries and issuing eight thousand grants each year through congressional appropriations and funding from partner countries, the program has provided scholarships to over four hundred thousand individuals, cementing its role as the strongest soft diplomacy tool for the US government. Globally, thirty-nine Fulbright alumni have served as heads of state or government of their home countries; sixty have won the Nobel Prize; and eighty-eight have won a total of ninety Pulitzer Prizes. Programs like the Fulbright have served as a vehicle for educating a generation of future world leaders in American values and principles, and for spreading American goodwill overseas when these students return to their home countries.

Countries and governments invest millions of dollars in educational and cultural exchange programs as a way to expand their influence as well as to train their young talent abroad. As someone who has spent many a waking hour figuring how to measure in hard numbers the impacts of such initiatives, I have often been asked the question: How do we know that government investments like Fulbright really work? Do they really have an impact beyond making their beneficiaries more worldly and culturally aware? What is the value to America and ordinary American citizens of bringing international students to the US, and why should their tax dollars pay for ensuring American goodwill globally?

In search of answers to these questions, I began investigating other scholarships and programs that have played a role in furthering America's influence and reputation. My research revealed something known as the "African airlift," a little-known episode in America's educational diplomacy that in the 1960s brought eight hundred postgraduate students on scholarships from Africa to the US. The program was the brainchild of Tom Mboya, a trade unionist and political leader in Kenya, in partnership with John F. Kennedy, who asked the Kennedy Family Foundation to pay for the airfare of 250 Kenyan scholars. Among those who are considered members of the "airlift generation" is the senior Barack Obama, President Obama's father. The airlift also included the Nobel Prize winner Wangari Maathai.

Excited to learn about the African airlift, I wanted to speak with someone who knew about the program. However, when I looked up the names of those who had arrived on the flights from Africa, most had died. But I then came across a BBC article that mentioned Susan Mboya, the daughter of Tom Mboya, the program's founder. I found her on LinkedIn and wrote to her. It was a shot in the dark; I never expected her to reply. But there was the response in my inbox two days later, saying she would be happy to speak with me about her father's legacy.

The Mboya family's story captures the impact of international education beyond what any set of numbers could possibly convey. Not only did Susan Mboya's father found the African airlift, but her mother had been an early beneficiary of the program who came to study at Western College for Women in Ohio (now part of Miami University). She then ended up marrying Tom Mboya.

So powerful was the influence of an American education in their home and circle that Susan Mboya describes her education path as "decidedly American." She obtained all her higher education degrees at US universities—the University of Connecticut and the Massachusetts College of Pharmacy and Health Sciences. She later encouraged all her nephews and nieces to study in the US, and even went on to found the Zawadi Africa Education Fund which gives underprivileged Kenyan girls an opportunity to study in the US. The idea her father had in the 1960s is continuing to have an impact on generations of Kenyan students today. For the US, too, it was clearly an investment well made.

I learned that scholarship programs were also effective for repairing our nation's ties with other countries and restoring mutual understanding. The tragedy of 9/11 inspired the launch of one of the most ambitious government-funded scholarship programs aimed at soft diplomacy. With fifteen of the nineteen hijackers identified as Saudi Arabian and highly negative public opinion about Saudis in the US, President George W. Bush and Saudi monarch Abdullah bin Abdulaziz Al Saud launched the

King Abdullah Scholarship Program four years after 9/11. It was envisioned that bringing more Saudi students to the US would educate the citizens of both countries about each other and help to mend US-Saudi relations. An added benefit of the Saudi program was that the students were fully and generously funded by their government, proving to be a windfall for US institutions that hosted the students. The program expanded rapidly, going from six thousand students to sixty thousand at its peak in 2015, making Saudi students one of the most visible foreign students on US campuses.

HAVING INTERNATIONAL students in the US isn't just a way for America to educate the world. It is ultimately the strongest form of influence, shaping the thinking and beliefs of the millions of students who have passed through the doors of an American campus, many of whom have returned to their home countries. The most obvious examples are the 570 current or former heads of foreign governments who have studied in America on US government–supported programs, prompting then Secretary of State Colin Powell to observe in 2001, "I can think of no more valuable asset to our country than the friendship of future world leaders who have been educated here."

It isn't just famous world leaders who carry the US banner abroad, and it isn't just the name-brand universities that have a strong reputation abroad. Small US colleges and universities have gained a mystique and prestige overseas when one or two international students who attended that institution become lifelong evangelists for it. It is the ordinary citizens, the everyday faculty and professionals who have returned home, for whom education is their connection to the US—whether through their own US alma mater, or because a relative or child is now studying in the US. They are the unintentional and unofficial global ambassadors for the US, spreading the country's educational influence far and wide and helping build and maintain bridges with the US.

When I was a student at the University of Delhi, most of the top professors had been educated in the US or the UK, and this number has only grown over time as a larger number of Asian students have returned to their home countries after studying in the US. These US-trained faculty have gone back to countries like India, China, and South Korea and have set up American-style universities, classrooms, and labs in their countries, hoping to offer their country the same world-class education they had received in the US. According to the academic, diplomat, and author, Kishore Mahbubani, a prescient Deng Xiaoping, the architect of modern China, once observed with hope: "Just wait until the forty thousand Chinese return from American universities."

Over forty years ago in 1978, Zhou Peiyuan, president of Peking University, established one of the earliest two-way educational exchanges between the US and China. Peiyuan himself had been a product of an international education experience, earning degrees from the University of Chicago and the California Institute of Technology, then returning to Princeton University in the 1930s to conduct research under Albert Einstein.

Today, the influence of an American-style education—particularly a liberal arts education—is evident all over the world from Ashesi University in Ghana (whose founder Patrick Awuah studied in the US as an international student) to the American

University in Kuwait and several universities in South Asia, including the Asian University for Women in Bangladesh and Ashoka University in India. In India, even the famed IITs—widely regarded as a quintessentially Indian academic brand—were influenced by American institutions such as MIT, with nine American institutions involved in setting up and shaping IIT Kanpur in the sixties. IIT Kanpur became the first institution to offer computer science education under the guidance of the Canadian American economist John Kenneth Galbraith.

Nowhere is the influence of American higher education more evident than in some of India's most innovative institutions today, including the Indian School of Business and Ashoka University. One of the visionaries behind these institutions is Dr. Pramath Raj Sinha, a self-described accidental founder and builder of world-class institutions in India. Pramath described to me how his fascination with American universities was sparked when he had the opportunity as a young man of seventeen to visit the University of California, Berkeley, and Stanford University—institutions that left a deep impression on him. He would go on to earn an undergraduate degree at the sought-after IIT-Kanpur and then a PhD in robotics at the University of Pennsylvania.

Some years later, when Pramath found himself back in India, working with the consulting firm of McKinsey & Co., which had just opened an office there, he remembered the impact his American education had had on him, a period of "five years of tremendous personal and intellectual growth that was transformational." When the opportunity presented itself, in an economically liberalized and thriving India, Pramath—along with other pioneers from business and academia—set up what would become the top-ranked Indian School of Business in 2001 and served as its founding dean. Pramath's next experiment was Ashoka University, an American-style liberal arts institution. One of Ashoka's other founders was also educated in the US as was one of its most high-profile vice chancellors, Pratap Bhanu Mehta, who taught at Harvard University and New York University. Ashoka is regarded as one of the most innovative and sought-after universities in India today, increasingly becoming the choice of some Indian students who might otherwise have gone abroad.

I asked Pramath what it was about an American education—that made-in-America brand—that had inspired him each time he had set up universities or educational programs in India. The answer came easily to him: it was the "student-centered" approach, in which students are treated with trust and dignity; the high quality of an American education, whether in teaching, content, or research; and the interdisciplinary nature of learning, which allows students to learn from each other. And last but not the least: it was the American way of going for both quality and scale, of going big and aspiring to be world-class.

Through countless conversations like these, I gradually realized that I too had become an enthusiastic advocate of American education. My journey had transformed me from being a critic of all things American into an ambassador for America, explaining American culture and values to friends and family in India as well as to new acquaintances from all around the world.

Whether it was apple pie, baseball, or the American ideals of freedom and free speech embodied in the Statue of Liberty and replicated in similar monuments around the world, the cultural influence of America is omnipresent. This is America's soft power, embodied in its most valuable global exports: its music, its movies, its religion, its magazines and literature, and the most influential export of all—its education. "Think about it," Ambassador Verma said to me, "Governments and ambassadors are extremely limited in the diplomacy tools they have at their disposal. It is people-to-people, educational and cultural ties that bring us together. America has been that place because we have the best universities."

Delivered at home through over four thousand universities and colleges while educating hundreds of thousands from other countries, an American-style education had carved a direct path into the minds, ideas, and hearts of the rest of the world. It was like the give and take of both jazz and Indian classical music: a symbiotic relationship between America and the rest of the world, in which each is nurtured by the other.

20

A United Nations on Campus

"What exactly do you do?" my father would ask of my new job. It was difficult to explain my work in the field of international education. Was it a subject or a discipline, given that such few universities offered a program of study in it? Was it a profession with a clear career path? Was it an exercise in diplomacy in which we were trying to connect people from one country with another through education? I couldn't quite figure out how to explain it.

For a time, I thought "international education" was a well-kept secret, known and understood only by a select few. But then I attended my first international education conference in San Francisco in 2006. Colorful banners hung from the ceiling and displays revolved overhead in the massive expo hall where the din of thousands of voices was so loud that it had become white noise. It was a marketplace of ideas but also one of concrete transactions, where various countries and universities hawked their educational appeal to each other and to students. *Study in the UK* was the tagline for the booth about the UK; *Come Discover Down Under*, beckoned the Australia booth, also vying with the UK.

As an international student at NCSU, I had never thought of

myself as part of a large population of similar students in the US, one served by an entire industry of campus-based professionals and an army of recruiters stationed all over the world. Now I learned that it is also an industry featuring a global whirlwind of conferences and trade shows, with some drawing upward of ten thousand attendees, each paying an average registration fee of almost $1,000. International education is serious business—an enterprise driven not just by the individual aspirations of students around the world, but also by the motivations and needs of countries like the US that host the students and the industry that has evolved to serve them, creating some 455,000 jobs in the process.

I had also been unaware of the massive, positive economic impact of international students in the US. Now, as I immersed myself deeper and deeper in the field as a professional, the lack of awareness of this impact on the part of ordinary Americans began to seem surprising. I once asked my neighbor Mary Barclay—a forty-six-year-old real estate professional and by all accounts an educated and informed American—whether she knew that international students brought in $44 billion dollars to the US.

"No," she said, in a tone of surprise. "I thought we were giving them all scholarships to come here."

My friend wasn't wrong: many international students, especially graduate students, rely on scholarships and support from their institutions to be able to study in the US. This was the case for me; I could not have afforded to study in the US were it not for my teaching assistantship. But in recent years, the balance has shifted. Today, most international students pay their own way for a US education. And even though I had an assistantship when I was an international student, I spent my modest income on all the same things that other Americans did: my rent check each month, my groceries and utilities, and the phone calls and airline tickets I paid for to remain connected to my family in India.

So great is the financial impact of international students today that US higher education is now one of America's top six service exports. America sells more college and university degrees to the rest of the world than either cars or medicines. Yet, unlike other exports, an American education never leaves the country, allowing US colleges, universities, and American society to reap the benefits of the presence of international students.

How much do US colleges and universities rely on international students? A lot, it turns out. International students often pay full freight for tuition, providing the extra revenue that US universities need to subsidize domestic students. At a time when US colleges and universities face shrinking budgets and the costs of a US education continue to soar, international students have been the necessary fuel that has propelled American colleges and universities.

It wasn't easy for me to uncover these little-known facts. When I became curious about the degree to which university budgets are dependent on international students, I discovered that this information is not easily available and most universities don't share their funding formulas. But some of the available numbers were staggering. The University of California at Davis derives some of the largest amounts of revenue from international students—$455 million in 2019. Because of the full tuition they pay, international undergraduate students at Purdue University add an additional $10 million in annual revenue. Like California, Texas and New York—two of the other states that also host the largest number of international students—have relied heavily on international and other out-of-state students to offset declines in per-student funding for public higher education.

On occasion, national crises have revealed just how dependent American colleges and universities are on international student fees to keep campuses and academic programs afloat. It happened after 9/11, when declining numbers of international students almost shuttered some science and engineering departments. In 2020, it happened again because of the COVID-19 pandemic. By some accounts, overall higher education enrollment in the US will decline by 15 percent and international enrollments will decline by a quarter due to the pandemic, resulting in an estimated shortfall of $23 billion for US institutions. The S&P Global has declared this a "material risk" for US colleges and universities. And in the UK, the expected drop in international students will cost universities $13.7 billion, a third of their total revenue.

The more I discovered about how essential international students are to the bottom lines of American universities, the more I wondered about the economics and purpose of higher education. I had always viewed education as a public good, an essential pillar for building strong societies. This is why smart countries invest a sizable portion of their budgets in educating their citizens. This was the understanding I grew up with in India, where the top universities were very competitive, but most of the large public institutions were highly subsidized. My education at the University of Delhi did not overburden my family, yet it had been an adequate—if not excellent—education. My mother could afford to send me to college in a large city and to cover all my tuition, fees, and living expenses on her modest professor's salary. We did not take loans, and nor did I have to work on the side to pay my bills, which freed me up to focus on my studies.

Now my research helped me to realize that the approach to higher education and its role in society varies across countries. In European countries like Germany, tuition for both domestic and international students is subsidized, but in countries like Australia, international students are big business. In 2019, Australian education exports were worth A\$37.6 billion, making higher education the country's largest service export. Similarly, international students added US\$31 billion to the United Kingdom's economy in 2018.

I also learned that, in recent years, the educational scene in India had begun to shift in the same direction. While the country does not have an international education industry and education at public institutions still remains largely affordable, many of the newer and most sought-after private institutions charge exorbitant fees that put them out of reach for many Indian students.

Meanwhile, in the US, while international students contribute billions to their institutions and communities, there is still a sense of unease about accepting that international education is an industry. The word "recruitment" remains a bit tainted, unlike in countries where higher education is seen as a consumer product and where there is no perceived moral dilemma about requiring international students to pay top dollar for the education they receive. It made me realize that if America is so reliant on international students, it is perhaps time to embrace this openly so that those outside the enclaves of colleges and universities can also appreciate the value those students provide.

International students are an asset and not a liability, but most Americans don't realize this.

AS I ABSORBED the full extent of how much American higher education and the economy rely on students from other countries, I couldn't help but wonder about a baffling contradiction: If students like me had over time contributed so much to America, why were we still viewed as a threat to American students?

Twenty years ago, David Phillips, the chair of the graduate program in my department at NC State, had felt that to allow me to remain on a teaching assistantship was to take away the opportunity from an American student. He had demanded that I give up my assistantship from the psychology department because I now had additional funding through my coop position. Fortunately, my advisor, Dr. Bishop—who was otherwise mild-mannered and avoided any type of conflict—stood up for me, loud and clear, reminding Dr. Phillips that he would never have asked an American student to choose one opportunity over the other. Why pick on me, one of the few international students in the entire department?

Yet even today the perception remains that international students are taking away college seats and opportunities from deserving American students. The evidence suggests the opposite: in most graduate programs, the presence of international students leads to increased domestic enrollments. But I learned through my conversations with middle-class American parents like Amanda Burns that such evidence is cold comfort to them. Amanda's sons attended top-rated public schools in New Jersey with full expectations of getting admission into top Ivy League institutions, only to find the reality to be quite different when admission time approached. It was hard enough to have to compete with students from around the US, but they were now vying against the best and brightest students from all over the world—a global talent pool that includes a growing number of affluent Asian students. Many of these Asian families were willing to pay top dollar for the best undergraduate education their money could buy.

Amanda expressed to me her frustration over this reality, and her concerns are not completely illegitimate: the share of international enrollments at elite private US institutions has continued to rise, even at a time when these institutions' overall admission rates have fallen. And it's true that a growing slice of their international students are well-heeled. Over the past ten years, more and more affluent young Chinese undergraduates, poised and worldly with their iPhones and branded clothes, have flooded American campuses, as have thousands of students from Saudi Arabia, flush with generous scholarship money and expensive cars to boot. Added to this has been the recent college admissions scandal which revealed that families of some American and Asian international students were offering bribes of millions of dollars to gain admission to top US colleges. It's no surprise that public opinion polls show that over half of Americans believe that international students are wealthy and are able to pursue advanced degrees because their families are able to pay for their studies.

But I found this notion of wealthy international students—where they were spending hundreds and thousands of dollars in the US—hard to reconcile with my experience as a frugal student, where I had to count every dollar and every cup of coffee. That is still the case for many international students. For most students from poorer countries, the cost of surviving in the US as a student continues to be staggering. Eight out of ten students from India take out loans to study abroad, often creating significant financial burdens for their parents, many of whom must pledge their property as collateral for the loans. At the same time, more and more Indian students are defaulting on their loans because of their increasing inability to work in the US to pay off these loans. So the emerging stereotype of international students as wealthy interlopers taking classroom spots away from deserving Americans is simplistic and largely inaccurate, though it contains a kernel of truth.

THE CONTRIBUTION OF international students to the US goes far beyond money. They have an impact on our country that is deep and sustained over time, bearing fruit in the future and therefore difficult to measure. When I was part of the international student community almost a quarter century ago, I wondered what our American classmates were learning from us and was struck by how little they seemed to know about the world. I became their resident expert on Indian cuisine, offering restaurant recommendations in Raleigh. And through me and my fellow Indians, they also learned about India's social and geopolitical history, about ancient Indian civilizations, and about the vast divides between the developed and developing world.

Even though Sherry Duan came to the US as an international student in 2013, much after I did, her experiences were similar. I got to know Sherry when she was a student in the class I taught at Teachers College. Growing up as part of a generation in China that even from afar was immersed in American pop culture and lifestyle, Sherry decided early on in high school that she would study in the US and tried to imbibe everything about America, including its education. Yet when she arrived in the US she found that her American classmates' understanding of China was outdated and stuck in the 1970s or 1980s. She recalled the time an American classmate suggested that Sherry alleviate her homesickness by visiting the Chinatown in New York City. Realizing that the student thought that all of China looked like Chinatown, Sherry leveraged technology to dispel his stereotypes. She showed him examples of Chinese social media and WeChat, the wildly popular Chinese messaging site with over a billion monthly users. Her classmate was stunned to learn that commuters in China could ride the subway without their wallets because they could simply swipe the QR code on their phones—a technology breakthrough that has yet to make its way to the New York City subways.

Sherry's classmate's limited understanding of the world is not an anomaly. Only 42 percent of Americans hold a passport, as compared with 76 percent of citizens in England and Wales, and 66 percent in Canada. Eleven percent of Americans have never even traveled outside their home state, and only one in every ten American students will study abroad, where they can learn firsthand about other countries and cultures. So, while the world comes to American campuses and classrooms, Americans themselves venture out in very small numbers to study elsewhere.

I first put this down to simple pragmatism: if the US has the world's best colleges and universities, why would its students need to go anywhere else? But over time, I realized that, just as it was for international students, being able to study abroad is also a matter of finances for many American students. When families simply can't afford to send their children abroad, international study remains the privilege of a select few.

One thing is clear: international students like me have helped bring the world to American campuses and classrooms. This is especially important with international students from countries like Iran whose histories and cultures have often been misunderstood, and where American students themselves aren't easily able to study. One of the few ways for Americans to learn about Iran is to have Iranian students study alongside them in class.

International students themselves also benefit from the global nature of US campuses. They have the opportunity to not only immerse themselves in American culture and academics but also have access to students from almost two hundred other countries—a veritable United Nations at their fingertips. So important are international students to creating a diverse learning environment on campus that most major rankings of universities today include the number of international students and scholars on campus as one measure of the institution's excellence and global prestige.

During all the years I had been busy making my way through the pipeline from international student to American professional, I had always felt a sense of gratitude for the opportunities that the US had given me; opportunities that were hard-won. I still feel that way. But as I learned more about how international education works, I began to realize that international students give as much as they receive, and that what they add to the US continues well beyond their commencement ceremony when they hold a cherished American diploma in their hands.

America Calling: A Troubled Tango

N ow that my career had made me a full-time researcher into international students and the benefits they bring to America, a funny thing happened: I began to notice students turned immigrants everywhere. Foreign-born Americans who have made powerful contributions to our nation's economy and culture are the faces of the American success story: Satya Nadella of Microsoft, Sundar Pichai of Alphabet (Google), Indra Nooyi, formerly of Pepsi, Fareed Zakaria of CNN, bestselling author Chimamanda Ngozi Adichie, noted architect I. M. Pei, and so many more—all first-generation immigrants who came to the US through the pathway of education. Each year, most of the American Nobel laureates are immigrants who arrived in the US as students. And two of America's most visible political leaders— Barack Obama and Kamala Harris—share not only a partial racial heritage but also having one or both parents who came to the US as international students.

Behind these famous personalities are all the other international students turned immigrants who move this country forward each day, from the immigrant doctors filling critical health care needs in areas of rural America where their US-born peers resist practicing to the numerous foreign-born faculty members and scientists at US colleges and universities. When it came to innovation and entrepreneurship, the most cherished of American ideals, one out of every four founders of a $1 billion US start-up first came to America as an international student. American companies founded by immigrants are worth an estimated $168 billion and have generated hundreds of thousands of US jobs.

Or consider Silicon Valley, which accounts for one-third of all venture capital investment in the United States. A third of Silicon Valley scientists and engineers are immigrants—most of whom arrived as international students—and nearly a quarter of the Valley's high-tech firms founded since 1980 are run by Chinese or Indian CEOs, America's "new immigrant entrepreneurs," the famed tech gurus who were creating jobs for workers in America, for Americans and foreigners alike.

The massive contributions of international students and aspiring immigrants at each step of the skilled immigration ladder were becoming increasingly clear to me. But at the same time I knew from my own experience and that of so many others how difficult it was to persist in the US. Students from all over the world were encouraged to come to the US to study, but then they were told to go home. It was like the push-and-pull of a dance: drawing a partner close, but then letting go; drawing them close, and then letting go. A tango between an individual's aspiration and a country's need.

Too often, when international students choose to stay, they face a downward spiral into a deep, dark abyss of rules, visas, delays, fear, and, worst of all, a crippling uncertainty about their future. It's an endless cycle of being tested and jumping through hoops—in the classroom as students, through immigration barriers such as restrictive work-study programs, and then as future immigrants. I finished my degree in record time not because I was particularly brilliant, but because I had no choice, tethered as I was to the stringent requirements imposed on international students. And I heard this sentiment from many students: the life of an international student is one of constant vigilance, leading to an inability to simply breathe and focus on their studies.

I HAVE A travel shoebox that contains every Indian passport I have owned since I was a child. All but one expired. The last one bears the bright red letters "CANCELLED" stamped across it, because I had to give up my Indian citizenship and passport when I became an American. I hold on to this canceled passport and look at it often because it is a reminder of my journey and the choices I have made—the same kinds of choices that the thousands of international students who graduate from US institutions are faced with.

Not every international student wants to remain in the US. Return rates are higher for European students, and some students on their governments' scholarships are required to go home. But most students stay in the US because education is a pathway to future opportunities. Yet this decision is not an easy one, as I well know. I think of all the times I was asked politely, "Do you plan to go back?" or was ordered to "go back to your country," making clear that I didn't belong. The decision to stay or to leave was not taken on a whim, but rather was a measured one, a reckoning and acceptance of what would be gained—opportunity and the American dream—but also all that would be forfeited: the lost comfort that there is always a home to which to return.

Just how large is the conversion rate of students to workers in the US economy and eventually to becoming American immigrants? In 1998—the year I finished my doctoral degree—two-thirds of international doctoral students who had completed their degrees alongside me were preparing to stay on in the US, with Indian and Chinese students having the highest "stay rates." Two decades later, 75 percent of all international doctoral students still plan to stay on in the US, with over 88 percent of Indian students planning to stay. And even though more Indian and Chinese students have returned home in recent years, drawn by opportunities at home, for every one US-educated Chinese expert who returns home, 1.4 Chinese scientists remain in the US.

The first stepping-stone in this journey is an obscure program known as Optional Practical Training (OPT). In 1998, almost seventeen thousand international students like me applied for OPT, which would allow us to work in the US for twelve months after completing our studies. But in 2008, Bill Gates of Microsoft, which is a top employer of foreign workers, stood before the US House of Representatives Committee on Science and Technology and testified about the importance of OPT and of giving international students more than a year to work in the US after their studies. Since then, OPT has been extended to a generous three years for international students in STEM fields (which is what most international students pursue in the US). Now that international students were able to stay on in the US longer, their participation in OPT quadrupled between 2008 and 2016.

But as with so many rules and regulations surrounding international students, OPT is also controversial and full of uncertainty since it was never created through legislation—a President's administration can alter the program with the flip of a switch. Those who believe that international students take away college seats from deserving American students and then take away American jobs also believe that the generous three-year OPT is a needless loophole. They say it provides a convenient workaround for the restrictive and lengthy H-1B work visa process—the next step in America's immigration pipeline.

Only sixty-five thousand H-1B visas are allotted each year. They run out within the first five days of accepting applications, leaving thousands of aspiring international students and their future employers stranded. An additional twenty thousand visas are allotted for students who have graduated from US colleges and universities, but even this number has not been enough to meet the demand.

The three-year OPT offers a safety net by giving students several more chances to try their luck at the H-1B lottery each year if they didn't succeed on the first try. It also allows the US to hold on to the global talent that arrives at its shores each year from all over the world which, if not retained, will promptly head to other competing nations in the West. And history has shown this to be true: every time countries like the US, the UK, and Australia have limited the ability of international students to stay and work, students have voted with their feet and gone to another country. And when such post-study work programs have been brought back, international students have returned, bringing with them their economic, social, and cultural capital.

One estimate suggests that the projected ripple effect on the

US economy of reducing OPT would be dire: a decrease in real US gross domestic product by about a quarter of a percentage point by 2028; a loss of 443,000 jobs over the next decade, including 255,000 jobs held by native-born US workers; and a seventeen-cent decline in the average real hourly wage by 2028. Restricting the ability of individual international students to stay and work in the US would end up penalizing all Americans.

According to public opinion polls, most Americans have a limited understanding of the tortuous visa process in the US. To check these data, I conducted an unscientific survey of my own.

I asked an American friend, Daniel Stevens, whether he had heard of these terms: F-1, OPT, H-1B. "I have no idea," he said, shrugging. "Are they food dyes or dangerous chemicals used in pesticides?"

Another friend wondered whether they were pejorative terms for immigrants, like FOB or ABCD. The most informed among them knew about the H-1B: "Isn't that the high-tech visa?" she asked. Most such visas do indeed go to workers in IT and STEM fields.

These are average, well-informed Americans who have barely any idea of what these terms mean, yet the eyes and ears of a country ten thousand miles away are keenly tuned into the details of America's educational and immigration policies. "Indian students not welcome in the US" and "US considers rescinding post-study work visa," scream typical headlines in India's newspapers and news channels. "Should Indian students still go to America with no work opportunities in sight?" In India, "H-1B" and "green card" are household terms, brought to the television sets of middle-class Indian families by reporters scrutinizing and analyzing every move and proposal of the latest American administration and what it might mean for thousands of Indian students and their families.

My own research into the H-1B visa program revealed that the visas were mostly going to Indians like me, then to Chinese students turned workers and those hired directly from China. Once intended as a temporary solution to fill the needs of US employers, the demand for H-1B workers soared in the twenty-first century. In fact, almost 1.8 million H-1B visas were issued between 2001 and 2015.

When I realized just how many H-1B visas were issued and how much the unmet demand was for such visas, it made me wonder whether there was some weight to the accusation that foreign workers—whether having arrived here as students or directly as workers—were taking science- and technology-related jobs away from Americans. Or was it the case that there simply weren't enough sufficiently trained Americans in the science and engineering fields in the first place? There was perhaps some truth to this, as a lesser-known fact is that a portion of the H-1B visa fee paid by employers seeking to hire foreign workers actually goes toward training US teachers and educating thousands of school students in the STEM fields, while also training American workers in critical technology fields with the hope that the US will eventually reduce its reliance on STEM talent from abroad.

By now I was a parent, and like any other immigrant in the US, I struggled with raising a child in a culture and context completely different from what I had known growing up. This applied to deeply ingrained assumptions and beliefs about education. What had been theoretical for me now became personal when I saw that the American attitude of rejection of STEM subjects and science and engineering careers begins early. While in many Asian countries a student interested in the sciences and mathematics is considered brainy and cool, in mainstream America the same student is often dismissed as a nerd, uncool, and a bit of an oddity.

Fast forward to college, and the result is a crisis in which fewer American students pursue the STEM fields at the undergraduate level as compared with their global counterparts. Further down the pipeline, half or more doctoral degrees awarded in the US in engineering, math, and computer science go to students from other countries, especially those from China, India, and South Korea. So large is America's reliance on international graduate students in science and engineering fields that Fareed Zakaria—once an international student to the US from India—wrote in a *Newsweek* magazine article that "the dirty little secret about America's scientific edge is that it's largely produced by foreigners and immigrants. Americans don't do science anymore."

There are those who challenge this perception. They claim there is no shortage of skilled labor within the US, and that tech companies merely want to bring wages down by hiring cheap labor from overseas. As a researcher, I turned to the precision of data. It turned out that, in occupations receiving the most H-1B requests, wage growth was actually stronger than the national average, and that a higher concentration of foreign workers in STEM fields boosts invention. The more H-1B visa holders there were in a given metro area, the larger the growth in invention (measured as patents) by both the largest immigrant groups —Indians and Chinese—and by US natives.

The data suggest that the ability of the US to innovate increases with the presence of skilled foreign workers and immigrant inventors. And then there is the overall financial impact: it is projected that an increase in H-1B visas could yield 1.3 million new jobs and add $158 billion to the US GDP by 2045.

FOR INTERNATIONAL students turning immigrants, the Holy Grail is the green card. My own experience with obtaining a green card had been long but relatively uncomplicated compared to the horror stories I heard all around me. This was because I was in a special category through which only a fraction get their green card. But for most, the process is long, tedious, and dehumanizing.

Since 2005, the demand for employment-based green cards has gone up significantly, and the waiting periods have become longer and longer, with many applications languishing for years. As the waiting period lengthens, so does the applicants' feeling of being indentured to their current employers. Even though in principle the immigration rules allow for someone with an active employment-based green card application to change jobs, the reality is quite different. Many applicants choose to remain in difficult, suboptimal employment situations because changing employers would mean resetting the dreaded green card clock, since being able to continue the green card process in an uninterrupted way was not a guarantee.

The situation has continued to worsen. As of 2020, there was a backlog of 1.2 million potential immigrants waiting for employment-based green cards, with most being Indians because of the strict quotas for the number of green cards that can go to applicants from a particular country. The shortest wait was for the highest skilled category of EB1 immigrants of extraordinary ability—the same category through which I had received my green card—with those from India in this category having to wait "only" eight years to receive their green cards. The worst backlog was for Indian workers applying through other categories: at current rates, they will have to wait almost ninety years for a green card. The Cato Institute estimates that almost 186,000 Indians would age and die while awaiting their green cards.

I heard the same stories wherever I turned: the ridiculous and impractical wait times during which life remained suspended; the inability to visit one's home country for fear of being denied reentry at the border; the necessity of walking away from professional and personal opportunities. There is no single estimate available of the impact of such delays on the potential losses to the US economy and the engines of science and innovation, but countless talented global aspirants report being tired of waiting and taking their knowledge and skills elsewhere.

When I asked Avi Vajpeyi, a young researcher in the highly specialized field of gravitational wave astronomy, about his decision to leave the US and move to Monash University in Australia for a PhD, his explanation was simple: "I told myself that I'm done with this. I don't want to do this anymore." Avi already had a green card, but after an inordinate wait and several failed attempts at obtaining a US citizenship that would allow him to pursue select jobs in the energy and scientific sector, he became frustrated and fled to Australia. The irony here was that his previous advisor from California Institute of Technology, Dr. Rory Smith, had also left the US and moved to Australia because of the challenge of getting a visa for the jobs he was offered in the US. The team at Monash is doing cutting-edge work in a field that won the Nobel Prize for Physics in 2017, and several of them had left the US because it was simply too difficult to stay on, to have to keep proving their worth in a country that didn't seem to value them. Yet, when I asked Avi if, all things being equal, he would have stayed in the US were it not for the immigration hurdles, his answer was, "Yes."

AS I REFLECTED on the experiences of Avi and Rory, I realized that the global competition for talent creates both winners and losers—when America loses, other countries win. But the reverse is also true: when America gains talent, other countries inevitably lose. Most international students come from countries in the developing world that can scarcely afford to lose their most talented young people. Countries in Africa are among those that have suffered most from this "brain drain." Is America at fault for "poaching" this youthful talent, or are their home countries to blame for failing to attract back their foreign-educated talent?

One result is the lingering sense of guilt, however misplaced, that many immigrants to the US feel. It's an emotion with which I continue to struggle, and this is perhaps the immigrant's cross to bear: the pursuit of individual gain weighed against the commitment to one's country. At some level I feel a failure over my inability to make a successful return to India, and so I've looked for ways to remain connected, to give back in some shape or form what my home country had given me for the first twenty-one years of my life. Many immigrants try to assuage this sense of guilt through philanthropic donations to the home country or by sending cash gifts—remittances—to family members at home.

I've also wondered why many countries don't do more to lure their young talent back home. The only countries that have been deliberate about this are China and South Korea, whose governments and institutions have launched strategic efforts to attract back their foreign-trained students and professionals. But India, as I well knew from my failed experiment of returning home, had done very little to engage in this type of "brain circulation."

As a result, the "brain gain" for the US continues. Indians today make up a large proportion of all scientists and engineers in the US, are represented prominently amongst the senior-most ranks of US faculty in many American colleges and universities, and are leading at least twelve top business schools in the US. In recent years the outflow of the best-educated and most talented Indians, be it students, professionals, doctors, or scientists, has only grown—while the reverse cash flows of remittances have diminished.

The massive wage gap between India and the US also contributes to the brain drain. An Indian academic in the US on an H-1B visa earns six times more than an Indian counterpart; in the field of management, an H-1B visa holder's salary is three times more; and in IT, an H-1B visa holder's salary is double that of an Indian counterpart. Or perhaps it is a capacity issue: with almost thirty-five million students in its overburdened colleges and universities, it isn't a high priority for India to either retain or attract back the thousands of Indians who have left the country in the recent past. There also do not seem to be enough jobs available in India to take advantage of the talent that might want to return home. About a third of India's youth aged fifteen to twenty-nine are neither employed nor enrolled in education and training. Where is the space then, for someone like me to return to India and find a job?

BACK IN CALIFORNIA, while I was waiting out my own immigrant ordeal, my roommate Rebecca had asked me outright what many Americans felt but were too polite to express: "Why are you here? We don't need you."

That question never seems to go away for international students and immigrants. It implies that we are outsiders taking away opportunities from deserving American students and displacing American workers. I had internalized this message, believing that I needed to somehow apologize for my presence, to make excuses for my accomplishments because they were wrongly acquired.

Since then, I've learned enough to reject the implied accusation. The evidence is very clear that American innovation, progress, and entrepreneurship since the 1960s has been driven largely by international students turned immigrants. Rather than displacing American students and workers, international students have helped create opportunities for all Americans. Behind countless successful enterprises is an immigrant, and behind most of these immigrants is the journey of education in America.

22

"Get Out of My Country"

My colleagues and I were gathered around a large conference table to discuss why the numbers of international students coming to the US seemed to be declining. Surveys were suggesting that students were no longer viewing the US as a friendly destination. Their experiences at immigration checkpoints seemed to be an issue.

"It can't possibly be that bad at the border," opined one of my American colleagues. "After all, we train immigration officers on how to handle visitors and to be welcoming."

I wondered whether to say something or to bite my tongue. He couldn't possibly know what someone who didn't look and sound American went through when entering the border. I recalled the time when, armed with a green card, I had returned to the US from a business trip to Mexico. There was nothing complicated about my reentry; after all, I had lived in the US now for over fifteen years. Yet when the immigration officer scrutinized my passport, I felt the fear I always feel when entering the US despite having all the legal paperwork, especially in today's America where being nonwhite and having a distinctly foreign accent are often considered signs of being the "other."

"What do you do?" the officer asked. I answered patiently,

but he seemed skeptical. He then asked to see my business card. "So, should I call you Dr. Bhandari?" he asked mockingly and with a faint trace of hostility. I didn't know what to say. He seemed to savor my discomfort and took his time stamping my passport.

My experience wasn't unique. Instead, it reflected the pattern of microaggressions that international students and other immigrants endure. The constant questioning of our presence, the constant doubt of our legitimacy. My native-born American colleagues had never had to contend with this. To always live with a sense of fear about being questioned or interrogated at the border.

Looking back, I now understood that 9/11 was the moment where everything changed for the five hundred thousand international students who were in the US that year. Before the terror attacks, the American public didn't care much about how international students were getting into the US and how many of them were enrolled at campuses across the country. But now, in the faces of Mohamed Atta and Hani Hanjour, two of the 9/11 hijackers, Americans saw the faces of all international students—wolves in sheep clothing, hiding their evil intentions under the noble guise of education. For too many Americans, "international student" and "F-1 visa" became synonymous with terrorism, and foreign students were catapulted into the public eye because one of the Saudi terrorists had been on an F-1 student visa. The fact that this was only the second time that someone on an international student visa—albeit an expired one— had been implicated in a major attack on American soil was scarcely considered. Newspaper headlines began to cite the numbers of students from different countries, and state governments began to question why their universities hosted so many foreign students on taxpayer dollars. For the first time in many years, Americans began to wonder: Do we even want these students on American soil? Where did they come from and why, and why were so many of them staying on? Why had 5,579 Saudi students been let in on these visas, and what did this say about all the other foreign students who were in the US?

I was not immersed in the world of international students when 9/11 occurred, so I asked those who had worked on US campuses then what the days and months following the attacks had felt like. They described it as a period of heightened scrutiny and fear: student visas were frozen, and international students were now constantly monitored and tracked through a $37 million Student Exchange and Visitor Information System (SEVIS). Unveiled as a supposed panacea for America's war against terror, the system required every student or visitor entering the US to be fingerprinted and photographed. Universities scrambled to meet the draconian requirements of the new system; any student who didn't report immediately to a campus upon arrival in the US was regarded as missing and posed a security threat.

As a result of the tightening of visa policies, the numbers of international students coming to the US fell for the first time in recent history. America's top-ranked graduate schools of engineering and sciences were the worst hit. Where once international students had dominated entire departments, classrooms now sat empty and deans worried whether graduate programs would even continue.

But the number of international students coming to the US began to recover slowly after 9/11. The appeal of an American education and the American dream endured despite terrorists, despite hostile border agents, and despite a growing wariness of international students in the US. It would be years before another crisis would hit the international education community, this one created by an unpredictable new American president.

ON FRIDAY, JANUARY 27, 2017, I received an urgent call. The brand-new Trump administration had issued a travel ban on people from seven Muslim countries, and students from those countries were caught in the crossfire. I rushed to tally the numbers of international students who would be affected. The sense of crisis brought me back to the morning of 9/11, more than fifteen years earlier. I felt the same sense of dread as I had then, except that I now understood how large a population of international students studied in the US. I also knew how damaging this travel ban would be not just to the students from those seven countries, but to America's image in the eyes of the world.

As the international education sector reeled from this latest blow, universities scrambled to assist their stranded students from the affected countries. In the week following the travel ban, forty Nobel laureates and over twenty thousand professors on American campuses mobilized to sign a petition against it, saying it would potentially destroy the international fabric of American higher education. Another online petition with over six thousand signatures from professors, scientists, and experts around the world called for a boycott of conferences in America. The message was clear: if America discriminated against people from disfavored countries, the world would stop bringing its knowledge and expertise to the US.

After a hard-won recovery following 9/11 and America's

reclaiming of its role as a destination of choice for the world's global talent, the damage had been done. The travel ban that January was the start of assault after assault on international students in the US over the next four years.

The history of international students and immigrants in America helps to explain what we experienced during the Trump administration. The fear of the "other" comes full circle every few decades and in every century. What happened beginning in 2017 was like the 1882 Chinese ban intended to halt the flow of the "yellow peril" to the US. Now, the growing distrust of foreign students was reflected not only in the so-called Muslim ban but also in repeated restrictions on Chinese students and scholars, driven by the largely unfounded fears that most Chinese students are spies, that they threaten national security and would take US scientific trade secrets and intellectual property back to China.

This seems ironic to me given how many Chinese students protect America by joining the US Army's Military Accessions Vital to National Interest (MAVNI) program which needs willing recruits with certain language and other skills and provides a fast-track to citizenship for non-citizens. I had not known much about the MAVNI program but learned about it from Sen Li who came to the US from China in 2013 to pursue his master's degree in biomedical engineering. Two years later, he was recruited into the MAVNI program which he saw as an opportunity to serve a country he had come to admire. But in 2017, the US government changed the rules for background checks for MAVNI enlistees and—despite having cleared all required checks initially—Sen Li found himself embroiled in delays and additional scrutiny because of pre-existing foreign contacts or having received foreign money (typically from family funds back in China that enabled him to study in the US). After years of waiting and uncertainty, he and other similar Chinese MAVNI recruits feared deportation because their international student status had elapsed, and they feared dire consequences if they returned to China. Sen was eventually able to file an asylum case in February 2019 and his court hearing is scheduled for January 2022.

TOO MANY AMERICANS have attitudes shaped by anti-immigrant beliefs. One recent poll shows that despite the heavy immigration rules and regulations surrounding international students, most Americans still believe that students from other countries are not vetted thoroughly enough and that they pose a security threat to the US. Yet the evidence reveals that very few international students of the millions who have come to the US over the past several years have been implicated in any crimes. From 1975 to 2017, 0.00017 percent of the 12.3 million student visas issued went to those who committed terrorist attacks. To put it another way, for every one terrorist who was issued a student visa, there were almost 590,000 international students who were not terrorists.

After 9/11, the severe backlash against students who looked Middle Eastern prompted the Harvard University–based Civil Rights Project to develop a guide for international students on racial profiling and hate crimes on campus. Sixteen years later, on February 22, 2017, an angry Adam Purinton yelled the words "Get out of my country," before shooting Srinivas Kuchibhotla and two other men in a small bar in Olathe, Kansas. Srinivas—

or Srini as he was affectionately known—was an Indian-born engineer in the US on an H-1B visa who had originally come to this country as an international student to attend the University of Texas at El Paso. The news of Srinivas's death reverberated across India. "US isn't a safe place, don't send your children there: Father of Indian engineer injured in Kansas shooting," ran the headline in the *Hindustan Times*, India's top English daily.

The attack on Kuchibhotla felt personal and visceral to me in a way that all those encounters at immigration checkpoints hadn't. It was one thing for an immigration officer to question me; the thought that I could potentially become the target of an armed and angry American was quite another.

"But this was just an isolated incident. There are so many hate crimes that don't involve international students," said my American friends in an attempt to appease my anxieties. And while it was true that in the larger scheme of things these incidents were few and far between and proportionally less than other crimes in the US, their influence was outsized, especially in the minds of parents viewing the news cycle from afar. Each international student was a potential diplomat for the US, a potential future world leader, a future university leader in India or China, carrying the dreams of their families, societies, and countries.

I quelled my emotions and instead sought the clear truth of numbers. After the Kuchibhotla episode, the numbers of international students coming to Kansas dropped. At Wichita State University, a 10 percent decline in the number of degree-bound international students on campus in the fall of 2017 left a nearly $1 million gap in the university's budget. Nationally, in 2018 most US colleges and universities reported continuing concerns about being able to attract international students, particularly in the Midwest and the central portions of the US—areas that are politically and socially conservative, are viewed as "Trump country," and have more relaxed gun laws. Since 2018, survey after survey has shown that while students around the world still nurture the dream of studying in the US, they worry about their personal safety, about racist attacks and gun violence. And this is especially true for students of color or those who are Muslim.

On a visit to India the winter after the 2017 travel ban, I spoke with a Muslim friend of mine. Fauzia Khan belongs to upper-crust, cosmopolitan families in Pakistan and India, and she has studied abroad herself, as have many members of her family. But despite their wealth and despite their eclectic, globe-trotting lifestyle, Fauzia is acutely aware of how her children might be treated as Muslims in the US. "I can afford to send my children wherever I want. Why would I pick the US?" To her, Canada seems much more appealing.

AS THE TRUMP years wore on, I found myself losing track of the long list of hostile proposals and executive orders targeting international students that were floated. Three versions of the Muslim ban; the threat of constricting or altogether eliminating work-study programs; visa restrictions against Iranian and Chinese students; placing strict limits on the duration of an international student's stay in the US while pursuing a degree . . . the list seemed endless. One estimate suggests that there have been a total of four hundred actions and proposals by the Trump administration that affect all forms of immigration, including international students in the US.

If students were feeling the brunt of the wave of hostile policies targeting them, so were university leaders. By mid-February 2018, one hundred colleges and universities across the US had come together under the #youarewelcomehere campaign, a social media–driven effort to reassure current and future international students that American campuses still welcomed them. The campaign gained traction and has since grown to include over 480 institutions and organizations that have put out over 250 videos of welcome and are also offering scholarships to international students.

Then, in July 2020, at the peak of a pandemic that had already crippled US universities, the Trump administration launched its most damaging attack against international students in the US, ordering that all current and future international students stay away from the US if their campuses were to offer online classes only. The US higher education sector convulsed, then coalesced, and several high-profile universities and organizations filed lawsuits. The proposal was eventually rescinded, but the damage had already been done in the minds of students and their families.

Every proposal to restrict or exclude international students has created a larger void between the US and the rest of the world. By the end of the Trump era, global opinion of the US had sunk to its lowest level in recent history. There was a pervasive sense of fatigue. I asked Hala, a student from Jordan, how she felt. "I'm just tired," she said. "I always wanted to come to America. I worked so hard—all those exams, the interviews. I thought the hard part was over, but now this." And for the first time, there was a palpable anger amongst current international students in the US. After all that they had invested in coming to America, all the money they had spent, and all the rules that they had dutifully followed, they had expected to be treated better. Many students found themselves asking the unavoidable question: Is a US education still worth it?

Yet, from where I stand, I know this to be true: international students have grit and are unfazed because they are used to struggles and upheavals and dealing with ruptures in their daily lives, be it fleeing to seek refuge elsewhere, facing health crises, or coping with domestic terrorism. And the arc of history shows us that a student's quest always recovers because of the strong desire to seek something better, to learn and go beyond. Like a phoenix rising from the ashes.

Epilogue

A s I write this epilogue in the first half of 2021, the world has changed dramatically. A raging pandemic has swept through the world, destroying industries, livelihoods, and social systems in its wake, while taking vast numbers of individual lives and forcing a reckoning of human existence in the twenty-first century. The US has also held an historic election that overturned the Trump administration. About half of America feels hopeful and is poised to "build back better." The country has also elected a vice president who represents many firsts: the first female vice president, the first vice president of Indian American and African American descent, and the first second-generation immigrant to occupy the role.

Yet the sense of optimism is cautious. The US remains a deeply divided nation. The destructive forces that have roiled American society were laid bare in 2020—the escalating xenophobia reflected in increasingly draconian immigration policies, and the social, racial, and economic inequities that have simmered just beneath the surface all these years and that boiled over when the pandemic exposed the underbelly of America. The American dream had clearly lost some of its sheen, and the world was watching.

One of my greatest challenges while completing this book was that everything I was writing about—education, immigration, and the hopes and dreams of young student migrants—was in a constant state of flux. In some ways 2020 created the perfect storm for the US when it comes to its appeal as a destination. The awful policies of the Trump administration were already having a damaging effect on the desire of international students to come to the US. New enrollments had been falling for three years, with much concern at the graduate level in science and engineering fields where international students in master's and doctoral programs fuel scientific progress and innovation in the US. Then came a virus that upended the very notion of movement and travel. Universities around the world were disrupted; US campuses shut down and students were asked to leave; national borders closed and flights were halted; economies tanked and families wondered whether they could still afford to send their child abroad; and US embassies pressed the pause button on issuing visas to students who were to come to the US.

Talking to international students, I heard horrifying stories of those who were stranded and unable to get on a flight back home. Many international students remained on campus, isolated in dorms and empty dining halls, unable to get around town because public transportation and Uber were no longer easily available. Then came the depression and the overwhelming sense of helplessness. Among Indian students, the pandemic made it obvious that many were not from elite and privileged backgrounds. Most were on frugal budgets, supported by families back home who themselves had suffered financially during the pandemic and couldn't send money across the seas. Some students had also lost their jobs. There were stories of students moving into a friend's or local guardian's frigid garage. A newly formed North American Association of Indian Students (NAAIS) stepped in to help and the Indian embassy in the US established a helpline and was fielding numerous desperate calls a day as students began to run out of money and food. And as often happens in such dire situations, in which struggling international students far from home become vulnerable prey for religious groups, Hindu extremist groups in the US swung into action to help Indian students with the hope of inciting them to join their ranks.

The pandemic also created an existential crisis for colleges and universities around the world, particularly for those that rely on large numbers of international students. Will technology and online learning ultimately replace the idea of a physical campus? These fears are legitimate, for an overseas education comes at a high cost for most students, and technology now offers much cheaper and faster options without ever having to leave home. But the events of 2020 have also revealed how the deep cultural immersion of an in-person education is irreplaceable, because a true education is about transformation—a process in which challenging ideas, debate, and analysis can lead to deeper understanding.

The COVID-19 pandemic will not last forever. History shows us that America's relationship with the rest of the world through the movement of students and scholars has survived twelve pandemics since the nineteenth century. Students who want to study abroad are incredibly resilient and the appeal of a made-in-America degree is astonishing. I have talked to many students this year, mainly Indian students, and survey after survey in 2020 has also shown that students still overwhelmingly pick the US as their most favored destination.

This is not wishful thinking; it's based on solid data. During the SARS outbreak of the early 2000s, the number of Chinese students fell temporarily, then recovered within three years.

Writing about this, Allan Goodman, the president and CEO of the Institute of International Education, which coincidentally began its work in international educational exchange during the Spanish flu pandemic of 1918–20, notes, "Planning for the 2021–22 academic year gives us all a chance to open academic doors wider than ever before. And so far, no pandemic has caused us to do so otherwise."

But let us not fool ourselves. The confluence of bad immigration policies and a health crisis will not simply be a blip, a bad nightmare from which we will all wake up and after which things will go back to normal. There will be important shifts and enduring impacts. Yes, students still overwhelmingly want to come to America, but in smaller numbers than before. The year of the pandemic has also proved to them that they have other options, including remaining home in their own universities and going to other countries that have shown the ability to deal better with a public health crisis and whose immigration policies feel friendlier. And then there is the role of technology, where "Zoom University" may not have constituted a holistic education, yet it made the acquisition of content and knowledge possible. "Whether America will remain attractive is an open question," shared a concerned Ambassador Verma. It means America will have to work even harder to attract the best and brightest to its shores.

Another important trend of 2020 was the belated nationwide embrace of the Black Lives Matter movement. Coverage of this trend allowed international students in the US to fully understand the society they were living in, but it also forced them to confront the invisible weight of racism that they carry from their own societies and cultures. Aryan D'Rozario, an Indian undergraduate student at the University of California, Santa Cruz, recalled that, while growing up, he had heard about Martin Luther King during a single class session in which the overarching message conveyed was that the civil rights movement of the 1960s represented the successful end of the struggle for African American rights. It was only after coming to the US that he realized that the struggle was far from over. It also forced Indian students like him to confront the narrative of being the model minority and having allowed themselves to become "whitewashed." During 2020, watching international students rallying and protesting alongside their African American classmates reminded me of how essential cultural exchange and understanding are, especially at a time when America is becoming increasingly nationalistic and isolationist: Americans need to understand the world, the world needs to understand America, and educational exchange is one powerful way to accomplish this goal.

The pandemic itself has been a testament to the importance of international students and immigrants, to these global migrants that seek the American dream. One of the first COVID-19 vaccines was developed by Moderna, whose immigrant cofounder, Noubar Afeyan, came to the US as an international student, as did its CEO, Stéphane Bancel. Two international students turned immigrants from Taiwan have also contributed significantly to lifting the US out of the pandemic: Taiyan Yang, the executive vice president of pharmaceutical development and manufacturing at Gilead, was behind the drug remdesivir, one of the few effective treatments for COVID-19; and Peter Tsai, a professor at the University of Tennessee, invented the N95 respiratory mask. And finally, there is Eric Yuan, the founder of Zoom. While Yuan did not come to the US as an international student, his struggles to obtain an H-1B work visa to come to the US are well-known in the annals of American immigration hurdles: he was denied a visa eight times before coming to America. Beyond these individual celebrities, immigrant doctors, many of whom came to the US as international students, have been at the forefront of the battle against COVID-19, often succumbing to its ravages. Over 28 percent of American physicians are from another country, as are over 56 percent of US doctoral-level researchers in life sciences and medicine. This is a moment for all Americans to pause and consider: Where would we be without these individuals who have chosen to call America home?

Yet it is exactly these sorts of individuals who are under threat in the US today, having been pushed away by the country's recent policies and messages. According to one estimate, due to the Trump administration's restrictive policies, legal immigration will have fallen by 49 percent between 2016 and 2021 and the country's labor force growth will be 59 percent lower. The US is currently on track to see the lowest enrollment of new international students since World War II, with much of this lost talent being diverted to competing destinations such as Canada and Australia. America's role as a global leader and its immense soft power hangs in the balance.

America must solve the puzzle of the higher education to immigration transition, but to do so requires, first and foremost, an honest conversation of the fundamental links between studying and staying on, and between opportunity and ambition. Some of my colleagues in the field of international education feel intrinsically uncomfortable about this, believing that international student flows fit best within the paradigm of exchange, with students who study in the US returning to their home countries to live and work. But this view matches neither the historical evidence nor the current reality. We tell students to follow their path to success wherever it may lead, to pursue individual excellence and opportunity. Why shouldn't the same message apply to international students?

The US and its colleges and universities will recover from the pandemic, but it will be a lot more difficult to recover from the damage of regressive immigration policies. They threaten something more fundamental: the very idea of America and the world's faith in America as a beacon, as a country of possibility. However, there are now groups like the Presidents' Alliance on Higher Education and Immigration, made up of university leaders in the US who recognize the strong link between higher education and immigration, and who champion the cause of balanced and comprehensive immigration reform. At the time of this writing, a new immigration bill has been introduced by the Biden administration that offers solutions to many of the problems that international students have encountered in the US—doing away with the unrealistic single-intent nature of the F-1 student visa; extending OPT, the post-study work program, for those awaiting H-1B approvals; and removing strict employment visa caps for doctoral graduates in the STEM fields, enabling the US to hold to American-trained talent that leaves the country. But as I have shown in this book, many of these issues have existed for years and then escalated under the previous administration. Despite these laudable efforts and the best intentions of the Biden-Harris administration, undoing the cumulative damage will take time and will require commitment from both sides of the aisle.

MY OWN JOURNEY as a student and immigrant in America has brought me to an interesting juncture. I am now also the mother of an eleven-year-old daughter who is a proud born-and-bred American. This has given me a different vantage point as I think about issues of education and migration, of the notion of home, and of raising a young girl in a country that has helped shape my identity as a woman. Hillary Clinton's loss in the 2016 election was a personal blow for little girls all over America. I still recall the day when after the election my crestfallen second-grader returned home and told me that a boy in her class had taunted her, saying, "We told you that a girl can't be president." Four years later, Kamala Harris's election as vice president has been a validation for hopeful girls and cynical women alike.

I also think about American education as a parent. Because I am the product of two systems, Indian and American, I am able to appreciate the weaknesses and strengths of each. Given my professional work, higher education is a frequent topic of conversation at our dinner table, and while I genuinely believe that the US has the world's best universities, I also know that young Americans like my daughter need to learn from different countries, histories, and cultures, as I have argued in this book. I also know that other countries have created world-class universities that are vying with America's Ivy Leagues.

What will I tell my daughter when she is ready to go to college? I will tell her that she needs to obtain some of her education in the US but that she should also venture abroad to expand her horizons and to learn more about herself and the rest of the world. I came to America to study; she may well choose to go to China, Australia, Germany, or even India.

I BEGAN MY journey in America as a newly arrived international student standing before an auditorium of undergraduate students in North Carolina. Some twenty-two years later, I stood before a class of graduate students at Columbia University in New York City, this time as a professor. It was a different classroom, a different university, a different era. But the students before me reminded me of my younger self. Half of them were international students from countries as dispersed as China, Vietnam, and Uruguay. They'd made a quantum leap in technology with their laptops and their cell phones, but some things remained the same. I saw familiar emotions in their faces: hope, anxiety, aspiration, and especially the desire to learn. Like me, many of them carried the weight of their family's aspirations.

The attraction of an American classroom has held strong over the years, and it holds strong today. But will it persist in the future? That will depend on America and whether it wants the world in its classrooms, in its streets, and in its homes. The question America has to answer for itself is not what it has meant to the world in the past, but what does it want to mean in the future.

Selected Bibliography

For this book I conducted extensive desk and secondary research, drawing upon scholarly and academic works; research reports and briefing papers by nonprofits, research centers, and think tanks; and articles in the global press. I also conducted interviews with current and former international students, higher education and immigration experts, diplomats, parents, and policy experts. Resources that were referenced across the entire book are listed below under Key Resources, while others are arranged by specific book section or chapter.

Key Resources

- All statistics relating to the numbers of international students in the US come from the *Open Doors Report on International Educational Exchange*, produced by the Institute of International Education (IIE) with support from the US Department of State's Bureau of Educational and Cultural Affairs (www.opendoorsdata.org).

- The book *International Students in American Colleges and Universities: A History* by T. B. Bevis and C. J. Lucas (Palgrave Macmillan, 2007) is an important and comprehensive overview of international students in the US.

- Statistics on the size and characteristics of the Asian American and Indian American population in the US come primarily from the Pew Research Center, as does analysis on H-1B issuances and OPT trends (www.pewresearch.org). See, in particular, the work of Neil Ruiz.

- For detailed information on the presence of foreign-born students and the foreign-born workforce in science and engineering fields in the US, see the National Science Board and National Science Foundation's *Science and Engineering Indicators* and its *Survey of Earned Doctorates* (https://ncses.nsf.gov/indicators).

- For extensive analysis and reports of the contributions of international students and skilled immigrants to US entrepreneurship, innovation, and competitiveness, see reports by the National Foundation for American Policy (www.nfap.org), in particular, reports by Stuart Anderson.

- For the latest news and updates relating to international students, the reporter Karin Fischer's regular newsletter, *Latitudes*, is an important source of current information pertaining to a wide range of issues that affect international students in the US. (https://latitudes.substack.com).

Chapter 1: Two Suitcases

Center for Immigration Studies. "Immigration-Related Statistics, 1993." https://cis.org/Report/ImmigrationRelated-Statistics-1993

Wang, Wei. "Testing the Validity of GRE Scores on Predicting Graduate Performance for Engineering Students." Public Access Theses and Dissertations from the College of Education and Human Sciences, 2013. https://digitalcommons.unl.edu/cehsdiss/192

Chapter 5: It Takes a Village

Zhao, Yilu. "Campus Evangelists Seek Out Foreign Students." *New York Times*, January 9, 2002. www.nytimes.com/2002/01/09/nyregion/campus-evangelists-seek-out-foreign-students.html

Chapter 8: Patel-Motel: Indians in America

Chakravorty, Sanjoy, Devesh Kapur, and Nirvikar Singh. *The Other One Percent: Indians in America*. New York: Oxford University Press, 2017.

Enzerink, Suzanne. "The 1917 Immigration Act That Presaged Trump's Muslim Ban." *JSTOR Daily*, April 12, 2017. https://daily.jstor.org/1917-immigration-law-presaged-trumps-muslim-ban/

Friedman, Thomas. *The World Is Flat: A Brief History of the Twentieth Century*. New York, NY: Farrar, Straus and Giroux, 2005.

Tichenor, Daniel. *Dividing Lines: The Politics of Immigration Control in America*. Princeton, NJ: Princeton University Press, 2002.

Zhao, Xiaojian and Edward J. W. Park, eds. *Asian Americans: An Encyclopedia of Social, Cultural, Economic, and Political History*. 3 vols. Santa Barbara, CA: Greenwood, 2013.

Mention of the full form of "ABCD" appears here: www.urbandictionary.com/define.php?term=ABCDEFGHIJKLMNOP and here: https://schott.blogs.nytimes.com/2011/05/04/abcd-2/

Chapter 9: History Lessons

British Council. *Postgraduate Student Mobility Trends to 2024*. London: British Council, 2014. www.britishcouncil.org/sites/default/files/postgraduate_mobility_trends_2024-october-14.pdf

Carrier, Peter, Eckhardt Fuchs and Torben Messinger. *The International Status of Education about the Holocaust: A Global Mapping of Textbooks and Curricula*. Paris: UNESCO and the Georg Eckert Institute for International Textbook Research, 2014. https://unesdoc.unesco.org/ark:/48223/pf0000228776

Dalrymple, William. "The Great Divide: The Violent Legacy of Indian Partition." *New Yorker*, June 29, 2015. www.newyorker.com/magazine/2015/06/29/the-great-divide-books-dalrymple

Hajari, Nisid. *Midnight's Furies: The Deadly Legacy of India's Partition.* New York, NY: Houghton Mifflin Harcourt, 2015.

Trines, Stefan. "Deja Vu? The Rise and Fall of Iranian Student Enrollments in the U.S." *World Education News and Reviews*, February 6, 2017. https://wenr.wes.org/2017/02/educating-iran-demographics-massification-and-missed-opportunities

Chapter 10: Coupon Queen

Fields, Samantha. "70% of College Students Graduate with Debt. How Did We Get Here?" *Marketplace*, September 30, 2019. www.marketplace.org/2019/09/30/70-of-college-students-graduate-with-debt-how-did-we-get-here/

Perez-Pena, Richard. "Smoothing the Path from Foreign Lips to American Ears." *New York Times*, August 28, 2020. www.nytimes.com/2012/08/29/education/college-helps-foreign-students-get-through-to-american-ears.html

Sanghvi, Disha. "Is the Education Loan Worth that Course Abroad?" *Mint*, February 19, 2019. www.livemint.com/money/personal-finance/is-the-education-loan-burden-worth-that-course-abroad-1550502001583.html

Chapter 12: Foreign and Female: A Complex Calculation

McChesney, Jasper. *Representation and Pay of Women of Color in the Higher Education Workforce.* A CUPA-HR Research Brief, 2018. www.cupahr.org/wp-content/uploads/CUPA-HR-Brief-Women-Of-Color.pdf

Rose, Stephen and Heidi Hartmann. *Still a Man's Labor Market: The Slowly Narrowing Gender Wage Gap*. Washington, DC: Institute for Women's Policy Research, 2018. https://iwpr.org/wp-content/uploads/2018/11/C474_IWPR-Still-a-Mans-Labor-Market-update-2018-1.pdf

Valenti, Jessica. "America's Rape Problem: We Refuse to Admit That There Is One." *The Nation*, January 4, 2013. www.thenation.com/article/americas-rape-problem-we-refuse-admit-there-one/

Chapter 14: A Temporary Arrangement

American Immigration Council. *The H-1B Visa Program: A Primer on the Program and Its Impact on Jobs, Wages, and the Economy*. American Immigration Council, 2020. www.americanimmigrationcouncil.org/research/h1b-visa-program-fact-sheet

US General Accounting Office. *H-1B Foreign Workers: Better Controls Needed to Help Employers and Protect Workers*. 2000. www.gao.gov/new.items/he00157.pdf

Chapter 15: The World Ends

LeBaron, Richard and Stefanie Hausheer. "Americans Must Do More to Welcome Saudi Scholarship Students." *US News and World Report*, March 1, 2013. www.usnews.com/opinion/blogs/world-report/2013/03/01/americans-must-do-more-to-welcome-saudi-scholarship-students.

US Government Publishing Office. *The 9/11 Commission Report: Final Report of the National Commission on Terrorist Attacks upon the United States (9/11 Report)*. 2004. www.govinfo.gov/app/details/GPO-911REPORT

Chapter 18: Made in America: The Lure of a US Degree

Bera, Anil. "Cosmopolitan Club, Tagores, and UIUC: A Brief History of 100 Years." *Cosmo Connections*, May 2006. https://sites.google.com/site/anilkbera/history-literature

Hindustan Association of America. *The Hindusthanee Student*. Vol II, No. 3. Berkeley, CA, 1915.

See the Yale Macmillan Center, Council on East Asian Studies for an overview of Yung Wing's time in the US. https://ceas.yale.edu/yung-wing

Chapter 19: Unofficial Ambassadors

Arndt, Richard T. and David L. Rubin, eds. *The Fulbright Difference 1948–1992 (Studies on Cultural Diplomacy and the Fulbright Experience)*. New Brunswick, NJ: Transaction Publishers, 1993.

Belair, Felix. "United States Has Secret Sonic Weapon—Jazz." *New York Times*, November 6, 1955. www.nytimes.com/1955/11/06/archives/united-states-has-secret-sonic-weaponjazz-secret-weapon-a-long-blue.html

Bonner, Alice. "U.S. and China Soon Begin Exchanging University Scholars." *Washington Post*, October 24, 1978. www.washingtonpost.com/archive/politics/1978/10/24/us-and-china-soon-begin-exchanging-university-scholars/3e7d12f3-6a30-49e9-8b22-d72a7cfe170b/

Kramer, Paul. "Is the World Our Campus? International Students and U.S. Global Power in the Long Twentieth Century." *Diplomatic History*, Vol. 33(5), 2009.

Lebovic, Sam. "From War Junk to Educational Exchange: The World War II Origins of the Fulbright Program and the Foundations of

American Cultural Globalism, 1945–1950." *Diplomatic History*, 37(2), 2013. https://doi.org/10.1093/dh/dht002

Rothmyer, Karen. "The African Airlift." *The Nation*, September 16, 2009. www.thenation.com/article/african-airlift/

US State Department Archive. *Statement on International Education Week 2001 by Secretary Colin L. Powell.* https://2001-2009.state.gov/secretary/former/powell/remarks/2001/4462.htm

Wheeler, Reginald, Henry King, and Alexander Davidson, eds. *The Foreign Student in America: A Study by the Commission on Survey of Foreign Students in the United States of America, under the Auspices of the Friendly Relations Committees of the Young Men's Christian Association and the Young Women's Christian Association.* New York: Association Press, 1925.

Mahbubani, Kishore. *Beyond the Age of Innocence: Rebuilding Trust Between America and the World.* New York: Public Affairs, 2005.

See https://us.fulbrightonline.org for a history of the Fulbright program as well as Fact Sheets about the program.

Chapter 20: A United Nations on Campus

American Council on Education. *Letter to Congress Regarding Higher Education, 2020.* www.acenet.edu/Documents/Letter-House-Higher-Ed-Supplemental-Request-040920.pdf

Jack, Andrew and Jamie Smyth. "Universities Face Budget Crisis as Foreign Students Dwindle." *Financial Review*, April 24, 2020. www.afr.com/policy/health-and-education/universities-face-budget-crisis-as-foreign-students-dwindle-20200422-p54m4d

Shih, Kevin. "Do International Students Crowd-Out or Cross-Subsidize Americans in Higher Education?" *Journal of Public Economics*, 156, 2017. https://doi.org/10.1016/j.jpubeco.2017.10.003

Chapter 21: America Calling: A Troubled Tango

Bier, David J. *Backlog for Skilled Immigrants Tops 1 Million: Over 200,000 Indians Could Die of Old Age While Awaiting Green Cards.* Immigration and Policy Brief No. 18: Cato Institute, 2020. www.cato.org/publications/immigration-research-policy-brief/ backlog-skilled-immigrants-tops-1-million-over

Business Roundtable. *The Economic Impact of Curbing the Optional Practical Training Program.* 2018. https://s3.amazonaws.com/brt.org/ BRT-OPTProgramReport_1.pdf

Cao, Cong, Jereon Baas, Caroline Wagner, and Koen Jonkers. "Returning Scientists and the Emergence of China's Science System." *Science and Public Policy*, Volume 47, Issue 2, April 2020. https:// doi.org/10.1093/scipol/scz056

Microsoft. *Bill Gates: Testimony before the Committee on Science and Technology, U.S. House of Representatives.* https://news.microsoft.com/ 2008/03/12/bill-gates-testimony-before-the-committee-on-science-and-technology-u-s-house-of-representatives/

Nowrasteh, Alex. "Don't Ban H-1B Workers: They Are Worth Their Weight in Innovation." Cato Institute Blog, May 14, 2020. www.cato.org/blog/dont-ban-h-1b-workers-they-are-worth-their-weight-patents

Rothwell, Jonathan T. and Neil Ruiz. *H-1B Visas and the STEM Shortage: A Research Brief.* 2013. http://dx.doi.org/10.2139/ssrn. 2262872

Wadhwa, Vivek, AnnaLee Saxenian, Ben Rissing, and G. Gereffi. *America's New Immigrant Entrepreneurs.* University of California, Berkeley, 2007. http://seipa.edu.pl/s/p/artykuly/90/906/ High%20tech%20entrepreneurs%20immigrants.pdf

Zakaria, Fareed. "Rejecting the Next Bill Gates." *Newsweek*, November 11, 2004. www.newsweek.com/rejecting-next-bill-gates-124639

Chapter 22: "Get Out of My Country"

Dunlap, David W. "135 Years Ago, Another Travel Ban Was in the News." *New York Times*, March 17, 2017. www.nytimes.com/2017/03/17/insider/chinese-exclusion-act-travel-ban.html

Horton, A. "The military is kicking out foreign recruits it needs—for having foreign ties." *The Washington Post*, July 30, 2019. www.washingtonpost.com/national-security/2019/07/30/military-is-kicking-out-foreign-recruits-it-needs-having-foreign-ties/

Nowrasteh, A. *Terrorists by Immigration Status and Nationality: A Risk Analysis, 1975–2017*. Policy Analysis No. 866: Cato Institute, 2019. https://www.cato.org/publications/policy-analysis/terrorists-immigration-status-nationality-risk-analysis-1975-2017

Epilogue

Goodman, Allan E. "When Pandemics End." ACE Higher Education Today Blog, June 29, 2020. www.higheredtoday.org/2020/06/29/when-pandemics-end/

Acknowledgments

Every book is as much about the story and journey within the book as it is about the journey of bringing an idea and a book to fruition. Along this path, there were so many who inspired and guided me, and who shared their stories with me. My thanks to Aryan D'Rozario, Avi Vajpeyi, Evgenia (Genia) Valuy, Sinan Zeino, Sen Li, Sherry Duan, and Wisdom Omuya—brilliant young aspirants, all—for their contributions to the book. Ambassador Richard Verma, Dr. Susan Mboya, Dr. Pramath Raj Sinha, Neil Ruiz, Anna Esaki-Smith, and Rohit Sareen generously shared their personal and professional perspectives.

Karl Weber, my wonderful editor, for immediately understanding the story I was trying to tell, and for helping bring the book to its finished form without sacrificing my original vision for it. My thanks to Brooke Warner, Samantha Strom, and the rest of the team at She Writes Press (SWP)—I am proud to be an SWP author and am deeply grateful, also, to the community of SWP authors who have been like an author and support group rolled into one! My excellent publicists, Marissa DeCuir and Simone Jung of Books Forward, worked tirelessly to bring the book and its message to a wider audience.

A deep gratitude to an international education leader and my mentor, Peggy Blumenthal, without whom I would have never had the opportunity to learn about international students in the first place; and to Jane Polin who has supported me in my personal and professional journey through her invaluable friendship and mentorship. My thanks also to Miriam Feldblum who leads the Presidents' Alliance on Higher Education and Immigration which tries to tackle exactly the sorts of issues I have raised in the book, and who generously invited me to serve as a Senior Advisor to the Alliance. This experience gave me important insights that are reflected in the book.

Last and most importantly, my family. My father, Arvind Bhandari, is no more, but I want to acknowledge the aspirations he held for me and that I have written about in this book. My deepest gratitude is reserved for my mother, Sudha Bhandari Anand. Writers are often asked about their writing process or routine, but as a parent I rarely had the luxury of dedicated writing time. When my responsibilities precluded the solitude of a writer's residency, my mother helped create that necessary space at home by taking over all those household chores that distract from focused writing. But she is also the one closest to the book, having been its first editor and critic, applying to it her expertise as an English professor. In many ways this book is as much hers as mine. And finally, my optimistic and resilient daughter, Zoya Anand Bhandari, whose frequent question, "So, what's happening with the book?" is the push and encouragement I needed to keep me going, and who patiently kept herself occupied as I worked to get the book to the finish line.

About the Author

Photo credit: Nicole Lebensor. Angulo

A former international student from India to the US and an Indian American immigrant, Rajika Bhandari is an international higher education expert, a widely published author, and a sought-after speaker on issues of international education, skilled immigrants, and educational and cultural diplomacy. An author of five academic books and one previous nonfiction book, *The Raj on the Move: Story of the Dak Bungalow*, Dr. Bhandari is quoted frequently in the global press, including in *The New York Times*, *The Washington Post*, *The Wall Street Journal*, NPR, *The Times of India* and *Quartz*, and her writing has appeared in the *Guardian*, the *Chronicle of Higher Education*, *HuffPost*, *University World News*, *Times Higher Education*, and the *Diplomatic Courier*, among others. She lives outside New York City.

www.rajikabhandari.com

SELECTED TITLES FROM SHE WRITES PRESS

She Writes Press is an independent publishing company
founded to serve women writers everywhere.
Visit us at www.shewritespress.com.

At the Narrow Waist of the World: A Memoir by Marlena Maduro Baraf.
$16.95, 978-1-63152-588-9. In this lush and vivid coming-of-age
memoir about a mother's mental illness and the healing power of a
loving Jewish and Hispanic extended family, young Marlena must
pull away from her mother, leave her Panama home, and navigate the
transition to an American world.

How Sweet the Bitter Soup: A Memoir by Lori Qian. $16.95,
978-1-63152-614-5. After accepting an exciting job offer—teaching
at a prestigious school in China—Lori found herself in Guangzhou,
China, where she fell in love with the culture and with a man from a
tiny town in Hubei province. What followed was a transformative
adventure—one that will inspire readers to use the bitter to make life
even sweeter.

*Her Name Is Kaur: Sikh American Women Write About Love, Courage,
and Faith* edited by Meeta Kaur. $17.95, 978-1-93831-470-4. An eye-
opening, multifaceted collection of essays by Sikh American women
exploring the concept of love in the context of the modern landscape
and influences that shape their lives.

In the Game: The Highs and Lows of a Trailblazing Trial Lawyer by Peggy
Garrity. $16.95, 978-1-63152-105-8. Admitted to the California State
Bar in 1975—when less than 3 percent of lawyers were women—
Peggy Garrity refuses to choose between family and profession, and
succeeds at both beyond anything she could have imagined.

Notes from the Bottom of the World by Suzanne Adam. $16.95,
978-1-63152-415-8. In this heartfelt collection of sixty-three personal
essays, Adam considers how her American past and move to Chile
have shaped her life and enriched her worldview, and explores with
insight questions on aging, women's roles, spiritual life, friendship,
love, and writers who inspire.